AI-POWERED DATA TRANSFORMATION

Modern Solutions for Insurance and Beyond

PANKAJ PANT, ANSHUL KAUSHIK, SATYA PRAKASH, SOUMA BASU

AI-Powered Data Transformation: Modern Solutions for Insurance and Beyond

Pankaj Pant

Anshul Kaushik

Satya Prakash

Souma Basu

Published By: Buddha International Publications

Website: https://www.buddhapublications.com

E-mail: info@buddhapublications.com

Mobile: +91- 7011267635

Place: Delhi, Mumbai, Ludhiana, USA.

First Edition: 2025

MRP: 400/-INR

ISBN: 978-93-6872-685-2

Printed and bound at Repro India Ltd.

Foreword

The world of insurance and data transformation is undergoing a seismic shift, powered by the rise of Artificial Intelligence (AI), automation, and modern data engineering practices. This book is the outcome of a journey deeply rooted in exploring how data, when harnessed with intelligence and purpose, becomes the foundation for innovation across the U.S. insurance industry and beyond.

Over the last decade, insurers in the United States have grappled with legacy technologies, fragmented systems, and regulatory pressures. Yet, at the same time, they sit on some of the richest datasets in the economy policy records, claims notes, customer interactions, and risk models. The challenge and the opportunity lie in turning this data into a strategic asset. That is where AI-driven data transformation enters the stage.

This book brings together perspectives shaped by hands-on experiences in leading modernization programs across life, property & casualty (P&C), and health insurers in the U.S. We have witnessed firsthand how machine learning, natural language processing, and intelligent automation are reimagining processes once defined by manual mapping, outdated ETL tools, and slow compliance checks. From underwriting and claims management to fraud detection and regulatory reporting, AI is now the backbone of efficient, scalable, and customer-centric insurance operations.

Our focus goes beyond technology it is also about governance, compliance, and people. In highly regulated industries like insurance, financial services, and healthcare, AI must operate with transparency, explainability, and fairness. This book will highlight how U.S. regulations from NAIC and HIPAA to SEC and IRS standards shape the adoption of AI, and how organizations can navigate these guardrails while still achieving transformative results.

What makes this journey particularly exciting is that the story of AI in insurance is not just about tools and platforms. It is about building AI-ready organizations—training data scientists, rethinking workflows, and creating agile, cross-functional teams that can adapt to the pace of technological change. It is about combining technical depth with strategic foresight to ensure insurers are not just keeping up, but staying ahead.

In the chapters that follow, you will find a structured exploration:

- **Part I** lays the foundation, explaining the new data era, legacy system challenges, and the shift from manual to machine intelligence.
- **Part II** dives into core AI techniques like intelligent data mapping, cleansing, entity matching, and workflow automation, with concrete insurance examples.
- **Part III** moves into real-world implementations, showcasing case studies from life, P&C, healthcare, and government sectors in the U.S.
- **Part IV** addresses governance, compliance, and the road ahead, examining how insurers can build talent, ensure ethical AI, and prepare for the future with generative AI, blockchain, and IoT-driven analytics.

This book is written for practitioners, leaders, regulators, and students who want to understand not only how AI is reshaping insurance but also how to implement it responsibly and effectively. Whether you are a veteran of the industry or a newcomer eager to learn, we hope these insights, case studies, and strategies help you see the immense possibilities AI and automation bring to insurance and beyond.

AI and automation are not tomorrow's vision—they are today's reality. The transformation is already underway. Welcome to the journey of data, intelligence, and innovation in U.S. insurance.

Acknowledgment

This book, *AI-Powered Data Transformation: Modern Solutions for Insurance and Beyond*, is the result of dedicated exploration into the transformative role of artificial intelligence across multiple sectors. I wish to express my sincere gratitude to the professionals, researchers, and industry leaders whose work and insights provided the foundation for these discussions. Their contributions have been invaluable in shaping a resource that bridges both practical implementation and theoretical understanding.

We are deeply thankful to the organizations and practitioners who openly shared real-world experiences of applying AI in complex environments. Their willingness to highlight challenges, opportunities, and best practices enabled this book to go beyond abstract theory and present actionable knowledge for the target audience. This collaboration has enriched the depth and technical rigor of the case studies and deep-dives.

Special acknowledgment goes to the experts and advisors in governance, compliance, and regulatory frameworks. Their guidance ensured that this book not only addresses innovation but also emphasizes responsible deployment, accountability, and ethical alignment in AI-driven transformations. Their perspectives have been crucial in balancing technical progress with trust, safety, and compliance.

Finally, we'd extend my heartfelt appreciation to the readers and professionals who are the true audience of this work. It is my hope that this book empowers them to adopt AI responsibly, make informed decisions, and drive sustainable value in their industries. Without the curiosity and commitment of such audiences, works like this would have little meaning or impact.

Preface

Artificial Intelligence has rapidly evolved from being a futuristic concept to a transformative force redefining industries, business operations, and governance frameworks. This book, *Industry-Specific Use Cases, Technical Deep-Dives on AI Applications, Governance and Compliance Insights*, is designed to provide readers with a comprehensive understanding of how AI can be practically applied, critically evaluated, and responsibly managed in diverse organizational settings. It aims to bridge the gap between innovation and accountability, offering both technical detail and strategic perspective.

The first part of this book highlights industry-specific use cases, illustrating how AI technologies are revolutionizing sectors such as finance, insurance, healthcare, retail, and manufacturing. Each case study is grounded in real-world application, offering valuable lessons on opportunities, challenges, and measurable outcomes. By focusing on actual implementations, the book demonstrates how AI can generate tangible value when aligned with industry goals.

The second part delves into technical deep-dives, where readers will encounter detailed discussions on AI models, data strategies, automation pipelines, and system integrations. These sections are crafted to support practitioners and technical audiences seeking clarity on how to design, deploy, and optimize AI solutions. They also provide insights into the complexities of scaling AI responsibly in enterprise environments.

Finally, the book turns to governance and compliance, addressing one of the most pressing challenges of our time: how to ensure that AI is trustworthy, transparent, and aligned with regulatory frameworks. Readers will find guidance on ethical considerations, data protection, regulatory compliance, and risk management, making this work relevant not only for technologists but also for policymakers, regulators, and decision-makers. This preface sets the stage for a journey that combines innovation with responsibility—an approach vital for the sustainable growth of AI across industries.

Pankaj Pant

Anshul Kaushik

Satya Prakash

Souma Basu

Table of Content

PART-I

FOUNDATIONS OF MODERN DATA TRANSFORMATION

CHAPTER – 1

The New Data Era

The advent of a new data era is significant in the context of the radical change in the functioning of organizations, industries, and societies associated with the active development of digital information, the emergence of new high-tech technologies. The current environment is not limited by the past days of data use in terms of speed, scale and interconnectedness as opposed to the former days of data use which were limited to databases, retrospective reports. Cloud computing, artificial intelligence (AI), the Internet of Things (IoT) and real-time analytics have made data the lifeblood of decision-making and innovation. Each online interaction: a financial transaction, a social media post, a sensor reading data point feeds into a large ecosystem that keeps generating insights, transforming industries and defining value creation.

The democratization of the data also defines this period of time when it is not only available to the executive and specialists but also to employees, customers, and stakeholders of all levels. The shift of organizations to integrated, smart systems has been caused by the transition of siloed legacy systems to a system capable of supporting smooth flows of data and quick decision-making. The healthcare, finance, manufacturing, and retail industries in the U.S. are using these capabilities to revamp infrastructure, make services personal, and streamline operations. Data is no longer a passive document of activity, but it is a proactive force that drives predictive and prescriptive models and enables organizations to anticipate risks, capitalize on opportunities and benefit competitively.

1.1. DATA AS A STRATEGIC ASSET IN THE U.S. ECONOMY

Today, data is being considered a strategic asset in the modern U.S. economy as much as any other classic asset, e.g. labor, capital, and raw materials. Joining assets in a physical form, data has an inexhaustible potential of reuse, refinement, and value creation in a variety of spheres. The increasing digitization of business and commerce, healthcare, finance and government services has turned data into the foundation of innovation and competitiveness. In this regard, the United States is not merely producing some of the largest sets of data in the world, but is also leading the way in innovative structures to gather, store and process them. Data can be economically valuable because of its skill to reveal trends, anticipate the results, and streamline the processes leading to the further productivity, profitability, and future developments.

The best example of the incorporation of data in the aspect of strategic decision-making is in the U.S. through the enterprises of the private sector. Giant companies such as Amazon use consumer information to sharpen their recommendation systems, predict demand, and make supply chains more efficient to redefine retailing networks. The reason why Google is leading digital advertisement is its capability to handle huge volumes of search and behavioural data, giving businesses highly targeted marketing strategies. In the same way, Microsoft has been able to incorporate data-driven insights in its cloud and enterprise services to enable organizations to move towards digital-first models. In addition to the tech industry, even more traditional industries like automotive and agriculture are reinventing themselves with state-of-the-art analytics, IoT, and AI-driven insights, demonstrating how data cuts across even traditionally asset-intensive industries.

Data is a vital governance and policy tool at the national level. The federal authorities of the U.S., such as the Federal Reserve, the census bureau, and the department of health and human services rely on large scale data infrastructures in order to track the economic activity, measure social welfare, and direct public health response. As an illustration, in the case of COVID-19 pandemic, real-time monitoring of the rate of infections, hospital overcrowding, and vaccine distribution became possible with the help of data systems, which highlighted the importance of data in managing crises. The idea of financial stability and consumer protection is also closely linked to data-centric regulation, as a predictive analytics can help regulators to identify systemic risks and avert economic crunches. The government is able to make more precise, productive, and sensitive policies by taking evidence-based decisions based on data, so that policies are aligned with the national requirements.

1.2. DIGITAL TRANSFORMATION AND DATA DEPENDENCY ACROSS SECTORS

Digital transformation is now a characteristic of the U.S. economy; it changes the way industries work, engage with their customers, and develop value. This change is based on how organizations are capable of exploiting huge volumes of data and converting it into actionable information. The dependency on data has ceased being a choice to stay but a survival requirement because of the growing level of competition in the business world, companies that have not adjusted to the current trends of data dependency stand to be rendered irrelevant. Incorporating analytics, artificial intelligence, and automation into daily operations, U.S. organizations are not only moving past standard efficiency benefits but are also building whole new growth paradigms.

Figure 1: Digital Transformation

The data dependency in the healthcare sector has transformed the care of the patients and the efficiency of the systems. Electronic Health Records (EHRs) are the platform of data-centered health systems that give physicians full-patient histories, minimize medical errors, and enhance coordinated care. Predictive analytics can help hospitals to predict patient admission, optimize staffing in the hospital, and even predict disease outbreaks. Wearables and IoT-based health sensors can produce real-time data about the patient, which insurers and providers can use to promote preventive care and individual care plans. The move toward precision medicine, which is propelled by the genomic and clinical data, indicates the extent to which the digital transformation has become entrenched in the U.S. healthcare environment.

The business world of retail and financial services depict the business aspect of this dependence. With the help of customer buying history, online browsing and social media interactions, retailers are able to design hyper-personalized shopping experience and streamline supply chain logistics. Such corporations as Walmart and Amazon rely on predictive analytics and AI to predict consumer demand and make sure that the products are available at the right time. It is no less in financial services where the data is the backbone of fraud detection systems, algorithmic trading platforms, and credit risk models. This data dependence ensures activities are more secure, efficient and customer-focused and can adapt quickly to market changes.

1.3. INSURANCE AS A DATA-RICH INDUSTRY IN THE U.S.

The insurance industry is one of the most data-intensive in the U.S. economy since it relies on vast amounts of data to run its operations. Data underpins practically all activities, from policy underwriting and pricing to claims review and fraud detection. Insurers use demographics, credit reports, past claims, and behaviour patterns to assess risk and set premiums. Insurance is successful because it predicts future risks, therefore timely and reliable data is crucial. The computerization of client contacts and the rise of online services have expanded data availability and complexity, making risk model optimisation and efficiency conceivable for the first time.

New technologies like telematics, IoT, and wearable health monitors have expanded insurers' data. Auto insurers utilise telematics to track driving speed, distance, and braking behaviours to create usage-based insurance (UBI) models based on actual driving behaviour rather than demographics. In the same vein, health insurance firms are examining wearable device data to encourage preventive health measures and reward clients who meet fitness goals with premium discounts. Since data streams can now track risks and adjust policies in real time, these developments have made insurance more proactive than reactive.

At the same time, Insurtech startups are using big data, AI, and machine learning to create new products and challenge the insurance paradigm. Lemonade and Root Insurance use AI-based chatbots for claims processing, predictive risk management analytics, and mobile-first platforms to improve consumer interactions. The disruptors that created personalized and flexible insurance products that digital-native consumers adore are transparent and fast. Threat from competitors More traditional insurers is partnering with and acquiring Insurtech startups to accelerate their digital transition. The convergence of established industry players and agile start-ups shows how data is changing insurance market competitive dynamics.

1.4. THE SHIFT FROM ETL TO AI-AUGMENTED PIPELINES

Data management in U.S. companies relied on ETL pipelines. These pipelines were designed to access data from many sources, arrange it, and insert it into central databases or warehouses for analysis. ETL techniques were efficient but inflexible, slow, and batch-based, limiting their ability to respond to current data streams. As big data, IoT, and real-time analytics emerged, organisations found that traditional ETL could not provide quick insights. These systems were limited by latency, manual processing, and dynamic bottlenecks that slowed data-intensive industry innovation.

AI-enhanced pipelines reconfigure data input, processing, and analysis in the new data era. AI-based pipelines are permanent, dynamic, and can learn data patterns, unlike traditional ETL operations. These pipelines use machine learning algorithms to detect abnormalities, inconsistencies, and errors without human interaction. This improves data quality and saves data engineers time on cleanup and preparation. AI-enhanced systems can also infer missing data, build relationships between variables, and create new derived values to provide analytical insight to raw data.

This transformation is especially beneficial in areas that require real-time decision-making. AI pipelines constantly monitor transaction data for suspicious activity to detect fraud in the financial sector, reducing risks to institutions and clients. In retail and e-commerce, real-time data processing supports rapid personalization, which increases conversion rates by changing product suggestions as customers navigate. Similarly, AI-enhanced data pipelines in healthcare can blend patient history, wearable data, and laboratory findings in real time to help doctors diagnose patients faster and more accurately. The examples show how AI-powered pipelines may turn data infrastructure into a dynamic, responsive service.

Cloud computing companies like AWS, Microsoft Azure, and Google Cloud have helped accelerate this transformation by adding AI and machine learning to their data platforms. AWS Glue, Azure Synapse, and Google Dataflow automate data preparation, pipeline orchestration, and real-time analytics at scale. This cloud-based architecture eliminates the expense and complexity of old ETL methods and scales with data need. Thus, AI-enhanced pipelines promise a paradigm change to intelligent, dynamically developing, and future-capable data ecosystems that meet the needs of digital-native organisations in the U.S. economy.

Chapter – 2

Legacy Systems and Migration Challenges

Legacy systems, typically developed decades ago, still form the foundation of a lot of organizations in the United States, especially those in the banking, healthcare, government and insurance sectors. They were created to meet particular functions efficiently but not on the scale, flexibility, or speed required under the new data era. They frequently use old-fashioned programming languages, inflexible architecture and in-house infrastructure, and it is challenging to integrate with the latest digital platforms. Although they might continue to fulfil their desired purposes, legacy systems inhibit innovation, form silos, and limit real-time sharing of data, leaving organisations incapable of considering all emerging opportunities such as cloud and use of AI, and sophisticated analytics.

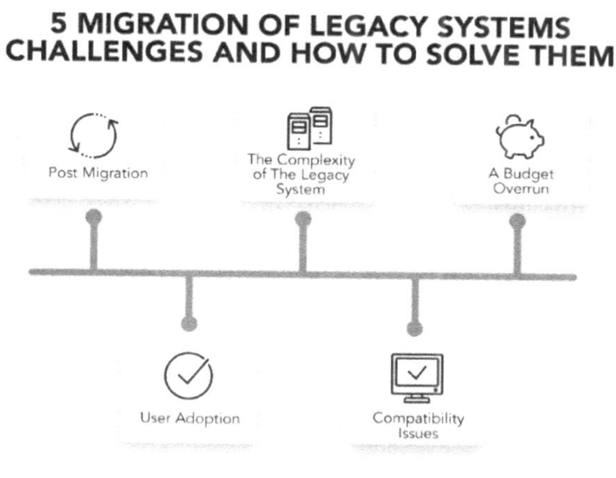

Figure 1: Legacy Systems and Migration Challenges

Changing the old systems to the new ones is difficult and not just technical. It can be expensive, time-intensive, and risky and particularly in systems that are of critical importance to the mission, downtime can cause havoc by disrupting vital services. This has been a problem in many organizations because the old applications might not be compatible with the new systems and this necessitates a lot of reengineering or redeveloping. Migration of data is a complicated process that includes the transfer of large datasets as well as cleaning, restructuring and data integrity assurance. Also, organizations might face the issue of the shortage of competent professionals who would be knowledgeable about the old technologies and the new platforms, and the transition may be even harder.

In addition to the technical and financial barriers, migration issues are both cultural and administrative. Employees who have been used to systems that have been in place might be resistant to change due to fear of their workflows to be disturbed and the new platforms having steep learning curves. The leadership teams need to handle change with some care therefore, they need to buy-in by training and use the phased adoption strategy in order to ensure buy-in. Nevertheless, the challenges do not negate the reality that modernization is necessary to ensure that organizations stay competitive because an organization that insists on legacy systems may end up incurring increased costs in maintenance, increased security threats, and lost opportunities in the ever-data-driven economy.

2.1. THE LANDSCAPE OF LEGACY TECH IN U.S. INSURANCE COMPANIES

The U.S. insurance industry was built on legacy IT platforms, most of them decades old. Traditional development using COBOL and other early programming languages created core systems on mainframes that were reliable and stable, helping insurers handle large data volumes. While these systems have served the industry well, they were built when products were simpler, customer demands were lower, and restrictions were lighter. However, complicated product structures, rising consumer expectations of digital services, and stricter regulatory norms have left legacy systems unprepared for the contemporary insurance environment.

Siloed policy, claim, and billing applications are a major challenge. Insurers must work in bits since such systems are rarely compatible. This causes staff to use manual workarounds and additional data entry, which increases administrative costs and slows operational effectiveness. Lack of seamless connection prohibits insurers from getting a holistic, real-time picture of client data for personalization, fraud detection, and risk assessment. Thus, insurers have struggled to deliver the digital-first, customer-centric experience customers expect from banking and e-commerce.

Another drawback is that legacy platforms cannot use cloud computing, AI, big data analytics, or APIs. They are increasingly significant in predictive modelling, customer engagement, and regulatory reporting. Inflexible old systems make incorporating new tools with pricey and sophisticated customizations difficult. Technological rigidity hinders innovation and digital transformation. Insurers that used outdated systems are behind Insurtech start-ups and competitors that use cloud-native solutions in a fast-paced market.

2.2. CHALLENGES IN POLICY, CLAIMS, AND BILLING SYSTEMS (LIFE, P&C, HEALTH)

The insurance companies work in various segments life, property and casualty (P&C) and health insurance with their respective complexities in operation. Although these segments have a few similarities in terms of process, technological needs and customer demands are vastly different. The systems used by these business divisions tend to be legacy-based and are increasingly unable to handle the requirement of the modern world of a fast-paced, data-driven setting thus present operation inefficiencies and sluggish innovation.

- **Policy Systems:** Insurance operations are supported by legacy policy administration systems, which process all aspects of the policy, such as issuance and renewal. But, such systems tend to be inflexible and hard and will not enable insurers to provide customized products, a bundled policy or usage-based insurance coverage. With the competitive nature where agility is paramount, insurers with old policy structures have been disadvantaged due to the inability to respond fast to the new market trends or consumer needs.
- **Claims Systems:** The other sphere that legacy systems have serious problems with is claims processing. Most conventional claims programs are heavy-manual with employees required to key in and check information in a variety of non-integrated systems. The method is time consuming and can error and it also makes it vulnerable to fraud. Clients are now demanding quicker settlement, transparency and proactive communication, especially in the health and P&C markets.
- **Billing Systems:** Insurance billing is a specialized operation that is complicated by diverse premium schemes, multi-line policies, instalment plans, and regulations. Early billing systems are not usually integrated on-demand with customer portals, payment gateways or reporting systems. This generates operational choke points such as billing mistakes, slow collections and customer complaints all of which lead to a poor customer experience.

2.3. RISKS OF MANUAL DATA MAPPING IN U.S. COMPLIANCE CONTEXT

Policy, claims, billing, and regulatory reporting in the U.S. insurance business involve huge amounts of data. Data is often structured (data bases, spread sheets) and unstructured (emails, PDFs, scanned documents). Insurers still manually map, reconcile, and evaluate data across outdated systems. In today's compliance-driven climate, the strategy is risky yet works effectively in small enterprises.

- **Possible errors and inconsistencies:** Manual data mapping is prone to human mistake. Even modest data entry or reconciliation errors might lead to incorrect regulatory reports, claims, or policy records. These errors may accumulate, causing system irregularities. Disparities in data quality make it difficult for insurers to produce actionable insights, financial, and operational reports.
- **Manual data mapping is laborious and inefficient:** Data extraction, validation, and use from one system to another requires time for employees. Due to huge teams handling regular mapping activities, this slows business operations and raises costs. Processing data slowly can also affect claims settlements, premium collection, and compliance reports, which affect efficiency and customer satisfaction.
- **Risk Auditing and Reporting:** Poor manual mapping exposes insurers to audit and reporting failures. Non-compliance, fines, and poor publicity can result from data mapping errors for Naic, SEC, and IRS reporting. Since its sector is highly regulated, even tiny deviations can result in compliance audits, fines, or litigation, strong and automated data management is essential.

- **Data Security Issues:** Sensitive data like health records, financial data, and Social Security numbers are often handled manually without automatic security or encryption. This increases data breaches, unauthorised access, and mistreatment, which can damage customer confidence and cost money to fix. As cybersecurity concerns rise, manual processes are vulnerable.
- **Concerns about scalability:** Data mapping manually is inefficient as insurers add products, switch to digital channels, or adopt new technology. Operation complexity increases error and delay risk. This hinders insurers' capacity to use higher-level analytics, AI-based insights, or cloud computing. Without automation, insurers risk being outpaced by more technologically advanced competition.

2.4. REGULATORY, PRIVACY, AND COMPLIANCE CONSTRAINTS (HIPAA, NAIC, SEC, IRS)

A complex and multi-layered regulatory structure governs US insurers' financial reporting, data protection, and operational compliance. These restrictions safeguard customers, stabilise the market, and ensure integrity in financial and insurance activity. Insurers may struggle to comply with these standards, especially if they use antiquated systems and manual procedures, which are usually unprepared for new requirements.

- **HIPAA:** HIPAA is a key foundation for data privacy in the US, particularly among health insurers. HIPAA mandates patient health information privacy, security, and confidentiality. Failure to comply can lead to costly fines, lawsuits, and bad press. Encryption, access controls, and audit trails are also required by HIPAA for insurers to protect sensitive data. Organisations with older systems without automatic protections or manual data handling are vulnerable to security attacks.

- **NAIC:** The NAIC provides a unified regulatory structure by creating model laws and standards among states. Solvency reporting, cybersecurity, consumer protection, and financial reporting are examples. Though states may apply NAIC models differently, insurers must have model-compliant operational processes. Accurate reporting, rapid disclosure, and effective risk management make compliance difficult, especially for firms with fragmented legacy systems or manual procedures that don't suit current compliance technologies.
- **SEC:** The SEC imposes strict financial transparency, corporate governance, and investment reporting requirements for publicly traded insurers. Insurers must ensure their financial reports are accurate, timely, and GAAP-compliant. With or without good intentions, misreporting can result in prosecution, investor mistrust, and market punishment. SEC compliance is complicated by manually reconciled or isolated outdated systems, which can lead to reporting errors and audit concerns.
- **IRS:** Insurance firms must comply with tax rules for premium collection, investment revenue, and retirement insurance products. Financial fines, audits, and extra scrutiny might result from reporting errors, delays, or inconsistencies. Legacy billing and accounting systems may struggle with IRS reporting standards, especially for multi-line items or cross-state activities. Automation and precise data mapping are essential to compliance.

Data controls, safety, and automatic compliance are needed in these setups. Legacy systems and manual methods make compliance tougher and put insurers at risk of legal obligations, regulator fines, and negative publicity.

CHAPTER – 3

From Manual to Machine Intelligence

The shift from manual to machine-based intelligence revolutionized how organisations use data. Manual data entry, reconciliation, and reporting took time and resources in traditional systems. Manual procedures are prone to human error, inconsistencies, and inefficiencies, especially when handling complex data. Manual operations hinder decision-making, raise expenses, and may violate regulations in insurance, finance, and health care. This limitation has driven organisations to pursue automated solutions to manage repetitive, rule-based tasks more efficiently and precisely.

Figure 1: From Manual to Machine Intelligence

AI and ML can automate simple and complex analytical processes. Traditional automation follows rules, whereas AI systems may react to changing data and make predictions or prescriptions. AI can automatically handle insurance claims, uncover fraudulent trends, and recommend policy modifications using real-time behaviour data. Finance Transaction data can also help AI programs find anomalies, improve portfolios, and predict market trends. By replacing manual labour with intelligent automation, firms can make faster, more accurate decisions.

Machine intelligence gives organisations better data insights and boosts innovation and competitiveness. Human experts can focus on strategic decision-making, creativity, and problem-solving while AI handles repetitive or computationally heavy jobs. The shift encourages data-driven decisions, reduces operational risk, and helps organisations scale up more efficiently. However, machine intelligence must be carefully designed, including workforce reskilling, ethical AI governance, and an effective infrastructure, to enhance organisational goals rather than destroy them. The change from manual to AI-based operations is crucial to making operations smarter, faster, and more resilient.

3.1. EVOLUTION OF DATA ENGINEERING PRACTICES IN THE U.S.

The US insurance market has evolved from data engineering to simple transaction processing to advanced analytics-based systems. First, insurers employed mainframe-based batch processing systems to extract, convert, and load (ETL) data at a set time. These systems could handle enormous volumes of structured data and perform rudimentary reporting and transaction processing. Their fixed, sluggish, and error-prone nature made them unsuitable for real-time decision-making or advanced analytics.

Data complexity and volume rose as the insurance sector grew. Insurance companies needed more flexible systems as digital channels arose and online consumer contact and regulatory compliance became necessary. This led to contemporary data warehousing and RDBMS. Insurance businesses may aggregate data from internal sources and gain more accurate business insights with the systems' faster data retrieval, storage, and reporting.

The rapid growth of heterogeneous data sources including IoT devices, telematics, mobile apps, social media interactions, and customer service platforms exposed conventional approaches' weaknesses. The old data systems couldn't mix structured and unstructured data, resulting in a disconnected database, manual reconciliations, and slower analytics. Insurers needed dynamically scalable architecture, many data formats, and near-real-time decision making to compete.

Insurers were interested in cloud computing, data lakes, and distributed processing platforms like Apache Hadoop or Spark. These technologies let enterprises absorb, store, and process massive amounts of structured and unstructured data. They provide storage and processing power for sophisticated analytics, predictive modelling, and real-time insights, which enable underwriting optimisation, fraud detection, claim automation, and customised customer contact. The shift from transaction-based operations to data-driven decision-making allows insurers to use modern data engineering approaches to achieve a competitive edge.

3.2. LIMITATIONS OF TRADITIONAL ETL TOOLS IN LARGE-SCALE INSURANCE SYSTEMS

The typical ETL tools have been used to integrate insurance data for decades. They centralise internal and external data in data warehouses for reporting and analysis. These technologies may perform well in a stable and predictable context, but in huge, modern insurance systems with complex data, they are difficult to use.

- **Scalability Issues:** IoT devices, telematics, mobile apps, and social media networks output high-volume, high-velocity data that standard ETL systems cannot handle. When insurers expand their product lines and digital platforms, data entry increases tremendously. This surge overwhelms conventional ETL pipelines, causing delays, resource use, and slower systems.

- **Limited Real-Time Processing:** In traditional ETL methods, data is processed in batches at a defined period, limiting real-time processing. The lack of real-time analytics for fraud detection, dynamic pricing, consumer personalization, and claims triaging is a disadvantage for insurers. Lack of real-time processing reduces competitiveness and consumer satisfaction since data-driven decisions are not possible.
- **Complex Maintenance and Adaptation:** ETL pipelines require manual coding, setup, and monitoring, making maintenance and adaptation complex. Technical work and time are often required to integrate new data sources, support regulatory changes, or enable new insurance products. This makes ETL pipeline maintenance and growth difficult, resulting in inefficiency and mistake.
- **Fragmented Data Integration:** Insurance data is diverse, structured, semi-structured, and unstructured, and provided by internal and external systems. Incomplete datasets, low-quality data, and no analytics result from typical ETL systems' inability to integrate all different types of data. Reporting, predictive modelling, and regulatory compliance may suffer from incomplete integration.
- **High Operational Costs:** Traditional ETL architectures require significant resources to maintain. Pipelines require specialised IT professionals, servers, and upkeep. This makes the old ETL less cost-effective in the current insurance sector, where scalability, flexibility, and speedy innovation are essential. Data volume and complexity are increasing operating costs.

These limits make next-generation data processing technologies essential. Cloud-native ETL, ELT, data streaming, and AI-inspired data pipelines can manage dynamic, massive, and complicated insurance data ecosystems. Insurance companies can get real-time insights, consolidation of heterogeneous data sources, lower operational expenditure, and stronger analytical applications by moving away from batch ETL.

3.3. WHERE AI FITS: FROM RULE-BASED TO LEARNING SYSTEMS

AI has transformed insurers' data processing, analysis, and decision-making. AI in insurance started out rule-based, automating repetitive tasks based on logic and business principles. Rule-based systems can prioritise claims, verify eligibility, or highlight basic irregularities based on thresholds. These technologies worked well in simple, repeatable workflows but were inflexible and unable to adapt to complicated situations and trends. Unstructured data including handwritten forms, emails, and customer service notes was not fully automated and limited.

By developing ML and deep learning systems, AI systems might learn from historical and real-time data and make more sophisticated insights and decisions. Unlike permanent rule-based systems, ML models can discover trends, abnormalities, and likely outcomes, such as fraudulent claims, hazardous policyholders, or pricing optimisation. These systems are always improving, and as they process more data, insurers can respond to changing market trends, customer behaviours, and regulations without manual reprogramming.

Other benefits of AI include processing unstructured and diverse data, which is growing common in insurance. Claims notes, emails, call transcripts, and social media interactions can be mapped, featured, and NLPed using AI. Insurers may extract useful information from sources that traditional rule-based systems cannot analyse, improving operational efficiency and enabling data-driven underwriting, claims, and customer service decisions.

AI allows reactive insurance processes to become proactive. Insurers use predictive analytics and adaptive learning to predict fraud, assess losses, and customize products and services. The shift from rigid rule-based framework to learning-oriented AI framework is crucial to modernizing insurance operations, operational agility, compliance, and client experience. Finally, AI gives insurers a dynamic, scalable structure to employ information across the company to turn difficult data into strategic value.

3.4. AI IN THE U.S. INSURANCE DATA LIFECYCLE

AI is gradually improving productivity, accuracy, and actionable insights throughout the insurance data lifecycle. AI can streamline data input and compliance reporting for insurers, enabling data-driven decision-making and agility.

- **Data Ingestion:** The first step in the insurance data lifecycle involves collecting and importing data from various sources. AI-driven systems may automatically detect information in databases, XML, JSON, and unstructured data including emails, claim notes, and social media posts. AI reduces manual ETL procedures, making data ingestion faster and more consistent and complete. This underpins downstream analytics.
- **Data Cleaning and Transformation:** To ensure accuracy and usefulness, data must be cleansed and changed after ingesting. Machine learning can automate manual tasks by detecting abnormalities, inconsistencies, and missing values. Artificial intelligence-led transformation improves data quality, allowing insurers to merge heterogeneous data

sources for sophisticated analytics. Higher data integrity affects prediction models and business insights reliability.

- **Data Analysis and Modelling:** AI can transform raw data into meaningful insights through predictive and prescriptive modelling. Insurers can predict claims, identify fraud, assess policyholder risk, and streamline underwriting. Machine learning, deep learning, and statistical modelling let AI find latent patterns and trends that conventional analytics miss. This helps insurers make proactive, educated decisions that boost operational efficiency and competitiveness.
- **Decision Support and Automation:** AI aids with decision support and automation, as well as human judgement in complex circumstances. AI may automatically process low-risk claims, reprice and underwrite risk-based premiums, or treat atypical instances. AI's repetitive tasks reduce processing time, errors, and free up workers to focus on strategic and customer-focused activities.
- **Compliance and Reporting:** The U.S. insurance market is highly regulated, making compliance crucial. AI can monitor transactions, discover irregularities, and generate audit-ready reports in real time to comply with HIPAA, NAIC, SEC, and IRS rules. Automated compliance monitoring reduces fines, improves data management, and provides unambiguous audit and regulatory reporting.

AI throughout the data lifecycle will help insurers make proactive decisions instead of reactive ones. AI will save operational costs, improve customer experience by speeding up and personalising services, and boost compliance. AI provides a flexible, intelligent platform to help insurers turn data into a strategic resource, boosting efficiency and creativity in a regulatory-heavy environment.

PART-II

CORE AI TECHNIQUES IN DATA TRANSFORMATION

CHAPTER – 4

AI For Intelligent Data Mapping

Intelligent data mapping AI is a ground breaking strategy to address complicated data integration issues in contemporary organisations. Manual or rule-driven traditional data mapping processes are a time-intensive, error-prone process that requires field and format matching across databases and systems. In other industries (insurance, finance, healthcare) where data is created by using multiple sources, such as policy systems, claims platforms, IoT devices, and customer interactions, manual mapping also can lead to inconsistencies, delays, and compliance risks. AI-based mapping of data is a form of automation in the process of identifying, aligning, and converting data on heterogeneous data sources using machine learning algorithms that guarantee accuracy and consistency and cut down on manual data handling by a significant margin.

The AI systems can intuitively deduce the connections among the data points, identify anomalies, and solve inconsistencies automatically by relying on such tools as natural language processing (NLP), pattern recognition, and predictive analytics. Indicatively, insurance, AI can be used to map customer data in the previous policy systems to the new digital platforms to make sure that the essential information such as coverage, premium, and claims history are registered accordingly. In the medical field, AI has the capacity to reconcile differences in coding and formatting to ensure a full and accurate medical history by matching patient records across multiple EHR systems. This not only speeds up the migration and integration project but also provides a high quality and reliable data upon which the decision-making and analytics is to be performed.

In addition to operational efficiency, AI data mapping leads to a better compliance with the regulatory regulations and risk management. Organizations in the U.S. are required to adhere to the highest standards including HIPAA, NAIC reporting, SEC and IRS rules in respect to data. Proper and automated data mapping facilitates the maintenance of audit trails, timely reporting, as well as diminishes the possibility of human error which may result in compliance violations or monetary fines. In addition, intelligent mapping helps in real-time data streams and dynamic updates so that organizations can respond promptly to any change in regulations or business requirements. Speed, accuracy, and adaptability allow AI on data mapping to be a vital feature in the move towards data-driven, intelligent enterprises.

4.1. WHAT IS DATA MAPPING? MANUAL VS. AUTOMATED IN U.S. ENTERPRISES

Enterprise data mapping is a very important step in data management and especially within the insurance sector in the U.S. It entails establishing the association of data fields in source systems to that of target systems. Ensuring that data is transferred, integrated and transformed consistently, accurately and seamlessly, a proper data mapping is essential in policy administration, claims processing, billing, risk assessment and regulatory reporting.

❖ Manual Data Mapping

Historically, data mapping was performed through the manually established methods of the analysts. This required people to:

- Analyze source and target systems to determine fields that match.
- Establish data type, format or unit transformation rules.
- Verify mappings to be accurate and complete.

Manual mapping might be suitable with a small-scale dataset or straightforward integrations but has a number of limitations:

- **Time-consuming**: Massive datasets take great hours to map.
- **Error-prone**: Human factors may cause inconsistency that may result in wrong reporting or non-compliance to regulations.
- **Difficult to scale**: Manual mapping cannot be sustained as business expands and systems proliferate, particularly in life, P&C, and health insurance settings where the products are complex, and volumes of data are large.

❖ Automated Data Mapping

Automated data mapping solutions based on AI are becoming more and more popular with modern insurance enterprises. Such systems use machine learning, pattern recognition and smart algorithms to:

- Identify source and target relationship automatically.
- Manage changing and dynamic data sets without massive human intervention.
- Check mappings to eliminate errors and inconsistency between systems.

Automated mapping provides multiple advantages over manual approaches:

- **Scalability**: Ability to work on extensive, complicated data.
- **Speed**: Streamlines integration and data transforming.
- **Accuracy**: Lessens human mistakes and enhances quality of data.

- **Flexibility**: Acclimates to new sources of data, new product lines, and new regulations.

❖ Significance in U.S. Insurance Enterprises

In U.S. insurance, data mapping underpins critical operational and compliance processes:

- **Life Insurance**: Mapping policies, riders and beneficiaries correctly.
- **Property & Casualty (P&C)**: Mapping risk attributes, coverages and claims data.
- **Health Insurance:** Mapping of patient data, claims and billing data in accordance with HIPAA.

Switching to automated data mapping will enable the insurers to become more operationally efficient, comply with regulation, and foster data-driven decision-making throughout the organization.

4.2. SCHEMA DISCOVERY WITH AI

Schema discovery the act of determining the structure, data types and the relationships in a dataset or in a source system. It is an initial process in integration of data because it allows organizations knowledge of how data will be organized then it can be mapped, transformed and analyzed. Schema discovery is necessary in insurance companies whose data are stored in both legacy and new applications and third-party systems to ensure that data stays consistent, good, and compliant.

Previously, schema was discovered through manual analysis by the data analysts which included study of databases, field names, and data relationship. It was slow, inaccurate and not always comparable, particularly where the data involved was large or complicated insurance products. The manual methods also had a hard time to keep up with the constant updates and structural changes in the data sources and thus the insurers found it hard to ensure consistency in integration and reporting processes.

AI has reinvented schema discovery since it automates identification of data structures. Machine learning algorithms are capable of processing large data sets to understand field names, discover data types, discover hierarchical relationships, as well as discover dependencies among tables or entities. As an illustration, AI can identify that the fields named DOB, Date of Birth and Birthdate all describe the same type of information and align them across the systems. This automation minimizes the human factor, accelerates the process of discovering, and the precision, even in very complex environments.

In practical terms, AI-based schema discovery enables the insurance companies to add new data sources (like new IoT or telematics feeds) to their systems without interfering with the current operations. It also aids in uniform mapping between different systems and this allows easier integration to administration of policy, claims processing, risk modelling and reporting on regulatory. Using AI to find the schema, insurers are able to speed up digital transformation efforts, improve data governance and have a scalable and reliable data ecosystem throughout the organization.

4.3. NLP FOR FIELD LABEL MATCHING AND SEMANTIC UNDERSTANDING

Natural Language Processing (NLP) has become a central component in the modern automated data mapping system because it enables systems to recognize field names, labels, and descriptions according to their semantic meaning, and not only according to an exact match of the string. In huge insurance business in the U.S., data tends to come in to the business by several different sources both internal and external all which have different names of similar concept. This incongruency causes manual mapping to be labour-intensive and liable to errors. To beat these hurdles, NLP takes into consideration the context and meaning of field labels so that one can correctly align systems in conflict.

A life insurance data may refer to the date of birth of a policy holder in various systems as DOB, Date of Birth or Birthdate. The old-type exact-match techniques would consider such fields unrelated and would have to be manually augmented. NLP algorithms, in their turn, process linguistic patterns and semantic relations in order to identify that these words indicate the same phenomenon. Through methods like tokenization, synonym detection, and embedding-based similarities, NLP can correctly map similar fields, as the conventions of naming in the legacy databases, in current applications, or in third-party data feeds are often wildly varying.

NLP is especially useful with unstructured and semi-structured data typical of insurance operations. The information stored in the fixed fields are usually policy notes, description of claims, emails, customer interaction and medical records, which have valuable information. NLP is able to extraction, identify meaningful concepts and map them to standard fields, and it is feasible to incorporate these differing datasets into analytics solutions and reporting tools or compliance processes, without having to work hard to do so.

NLP increases the accuracy and the scalability of integration processes by facilitating semantic comprehending in automated data mapping. The benefits of the technology to insurers include the need to do less human-based work, onboarding and data sources more quickly, and better quality data across systems. Finally, NLP-powered mapping assists in streamlined claims processing, policy management, detection of fraud, and compliance with regulations, enabling insurance companies to stay at a competitive advantage in the current information-focused world.

4.4. HANDLING COMPLEX MAPPINGS: HIERARCHICAL AND NESTED STRUCTURES

Complex hierarchical or embedded insurance information is always present. Example: A life insurance policy may have riders, beneficiaries, coverage conditions, and premium schedules. In P&C insurance, a property policy might include many risk factors, endorsements, and claims history for one policyholder. Traditional one-to-one or flat field mapping techniques cannot accurately portray these nested relationships. Data discrepancies, missing integration, and reporting inaccuracies can hurt regulated industries like insurance.

AI-based mapping solutions automatically discover complicated data hierarchies and layered structures to solve these issues. These systems recognised parent-child linkages, relationships, and repeating entities and map all data levels into target systems. AI can map a life insurance policy and detect riders and beneficiaries. This level of smart mapping preserves data integrity and context for downstream analytics and procedures.

Complex mappings are handled, improving data consistency between platforms. Insurance companies use legacy, cloud, and third-party systems. AI-based hierarchical mapping normalizes layered structures throughout the system of systems to simplify policy management, claims processing, and customer service integration. The AI mirrors multi-level relationships, reducing data duplication, misalignment, and loss.

In addition, automatic hierarchical mapping aids regulatory compliance and reporting. Proper layered data representation helps capture all policy sections, claims, and endorsements for audit and regulatory purposes. It supports complex analytics like risk assessment, fraud detection, and predictive modelling that require precise and levelled data. In conclusion, AI-based hierarchical and nest data mapping improves insurance data ecosystem efficiency, reduces human work, and boosts trust.

4.5. MAPPING FOR LIFE INSURANCE IN THE U.S.: PRODUCTS, RIDERS, POLICIES

The complexity in data mapping of life insurance is the level of multiple products, riders, beneficiaries and policy attributes. A typical life insurance policy is filled with numerous fields that consist of the coverage amounts, premium schedules, policy terms, conditions and optional riders. Proper mapping guarantees that such components are properly reflected in various systems, which reflects effective operations, regulatory compliance, and hassle-free customer services.

❖ **Policy Administration**

Data mapping is very essential in the policy administration process since the insurance companies need to capture all the policy characteristics in the internal systems. Proper mapping allows for:

- Stable display of coverage values, policy conditions, and optional riders in various platforms.
- Effective policy updates and endorsement as well as renewal processing.
- Less chance of policy documentation or system record errors, potentially impacting customer satisfaction or causing compliance problems.

❖ Claims Processing

The insurance claims in life insurance involve the accurate mapping of the considerations of beneficiaries, coverage and pay-out conditions. Accurate data mapping ensures:

- Proper beneficiary identification and entitlements.
- Appropriate distribution of coverage values in regard to policy and rider.
- Quick and improved claims approval and settlement, less time wastage and customer satisfaction. AI-based mapping minimizes human involvement in the map, which makes it accurate, consistent, and fast in the claims operation.

❖ Regulatory Reporting

The life insurers in U.S. have to be subjected to tough regulatory structures, such as NAIC requirements, and state-specific requirements. Data mapping ensures that:

- The policy and rider information is synchronized with reporting standards.
- Audits and compliance reporting of all needed data points is always done.
- Reporting systems are updated with changes in product structures or change of regulations without human effort.

❖ Role of AI in Life Insurance Data Mapping

AI-driven solutions simplify life insurance data mapping by:

- Fields between different systems automatically discovered.
- Paring the right policies, riders and beneficiaries.

- Managing product structures as they change, including new riders or policy features or coverage options.

Using AI, insurers can save manual labor, minimize errors, and increase the accuracy of data in areas of policy management, claims processing, and compliance reporting. This not only simplifies operations but also assists data-based decision-making and enhances compliance in an extremely regulated sector.

4.6. MAPPING FOR P&C IN THE U.S.: RISK ATTRIBUTES, COVERAGES, CLAIMS

The nature of Property and Casualty (P&C) insurance data is complex in terms of varying risk properties, cover structures, and deep-level claims data. Good data mapping between systems is of utmost importance to validate the efficiency in operation, regulation and in decision-making. P&C insurers can have data stored in legacy databases, cloud environments and third-party data, which can be tedious and error-prone when manually mapped. Intelligent solutions exist to automate and simplify these mapping procedures with AI and machine learning.

❖ Risk Attributes

One of the major components of P&C insurance is the identification and mapping of risk characteristics of policies. Risk attributes include:

- Property characteristics like the type of building, location, age and construction materials.
- Hazard factors such as exposure to natural disasters, the risk of fire and the liability risk.
- Liability exposures associated with third party coverage or agreement liabilities.

Proper mapping of these attributes will make the underwriting, pricing and risk assessment processes correlated across systems. AI algorithms can identify patterns within risk data, identify relationships, and manage hierarchical structures, which enhances accuracy and decreases the manual effort.

❖ **Coverages**

P&C policies are commonly characterized by various cover aspects that may include limits, deductibles, endorsements and exclusions. Mapping these accurately is critical to:

- Standardize policy information on administration, billing, and analytics systems.
- Automated claims adjudication support and avoid coverage mismatch.
- Empower accurate regulatory compliance and risk management reporting.

AI-based mapping Semantic understanding and pattern recognition are applied to compare coverage components across systems despite differences in the field labels or structure. This will make sure that every aspect of the policy is well understood and incorporated, which will improve the efficiency of operations.

❖ **Claims Data**

Claims processing in P&C insurance requires accurate mapping of:

- Claim submissions and incident reports.
- Payment amounts, adjustments, and settlement details.
- Status updates and documentation for audit trails and analytics.

AI-based mapping may identify intricate relations among claims, policies, and risk features, thereby preserving data quality and providing more rapid processing. It also helps in fraud detection, predictive analytics, and reporting and lessens errors and enhances customer satisfaction.

❖ Role of AI and Machine Learning

AI and machine learning enhance P&C data mapping by:

- Identifying hierarchical links among embedded entities such as multiple coverages or claims on one policy.
- Identifying semantic similarity between field labels and intersystem values.
- Automation of repetitive mapping, human intervention, operational and risk of error reduction.

P&C insurers can do more with AI, like obtain better data quality, quicker claims, less biased risk, and sound regulatory adherence, to establish a technology- scalable and dependable data environment throughout the organization.

CHAPTER – 5

Smart Data Cleansing and Normalization

Cleansing and normalization of data are highly important operations in the modern data management that guarantees that data is correct, dependable, and prepared to be analyzed. Traditional systems may provide a variety of data providers, legacy applications, IoT devices, customer interactions, or external databases and this data can be inaccurate, duplicate, lack value, or have inconsistent formatting. Such problems can hinder decision-making, wrong insights, and compliance risks unless these problems are properly cleansed and normalized. Smart data cleansing applies AI and machine learning to automatically identify anomalies, remove errors and standardize datasets, which dramatically reduces the amount of manual intervention and enhances the quality of data overall.

Figure 1: Data Cleansing

Normalization is used to augment cleansing and ensure that data is converted into a uniform structure and format across systems so that it can be used in analytics and integration. An example is that addresses, dates, currency formatting, and product codes can differ among datasets; normalization will make them conform to one standard. The normalized data enables organizations in all industries such as insurance, healthcare, and finance to combine information of various sources, risk assessment with accuracy, and create regulatory reports easily. Normalization tools powered by AI can also be trained over time to adapt to new streams of data and adjust to business requirements and updated business rules, thereby increasing scalability and minimizing repetitive manual labor.

In addition to operational efficiency, smart data cleansing and normalization have a direct influence on compliance, governance, and decision-making. It is important to compare the standards that have to be met by organizations in the U.S. HIPAA requirements of healthcare data, NAIC reporting requirements of insurance, or SEC or IRS requirements of financial records. Data integrity, generation of credible audit trails and reduced human errors are ensured through automated cleansing and normalization to ensure compliance with regulatory requirements. Moreover, quality, standardized data allows real-time data analytics, predictive modelling and machine learning solutions to convert raw data into actionable insights.

5.1. OVERVIEW OF DATA QUALITY ISSUES IN U.S. INSURANCE FIRMS

Data quality is a major issue to U.S. insurance companies, who are tasked with managing significant amounts of heterogeneous and complex data in life, property and casualty (P&C), and health insurance. The data must be of high quality to be compliant with regulations, effective operations and customer trust. Nevertheless, insurers are confronted with numerous difficulties when it comes to the accuracy, completeness, and consistence of data in legacy systems, cloud applications, and third-party sources of data. These difficulties can cause problems in decision-making, analytics, and reporting and result in losses of funds and reputation in case they remain unaddressed.

- **Incomplete or Missing Data:** One of the most frequent problems of insurance systems is incomplete or missing data. Fields can be absent in policyholder records, claims or risk attributes, which can compromise the accuracy of analytics, risk assessment, and reporting. As an illustration, the absence of beneficiary details or coverage pieces may slow down the claims and result in non-adherence. Moreover, employees might end up wasting much time in referencing or fixing missing records manually leading to inefficiency and high costs of operations.
- **Inconsistent Data:** Data inconsistency exists when various systems apply different names, different format, or different coding. An example here is the date of birth that can be written as Date of Birth in one system, and DOB in another, as well as, Birth Date in the third system. Such differences complicate cross-system integration and may cause misalignment of reporting, analytics mistakes, and regulatory compliance difficulties. In the absence of standardization, there will be huge barriers in consolidating data to support underwriting, claims analysis, and business intelligence projects by insurers.
- **Duplicate Records:** One more common problem is duplicate records in insurance data management. There can be many records of the same policy holder, claim or policy that distort analytics, introduce operational inefficiencies and present compliance risk. Indicatively, duplication of claims records might result in overpayment, misreporting of risk or reporting these to the regulators. Locating and merging duplicates is essential in ensuring the correct data, facilitation of operations and elimination of unnecessary processing.

- **Erroneous Data:** Data errors may occur due to errors in data entry or older information or improper evaluation of a risk. Such miscalculations can be very detrimental in the insurance processes. This is because inaccurate data can lead to incorrect pricing of policies, wrongful settlement of claims or poor actuarial models. Besides influencing financial accuracy, bad data quality can influence customer satisfaction, where the clients might get delays or errors when using the policy or handling claims.
- **Integration Challenges:** Insurance companies normally have a mix of legacy platforms, cloud platforms, and third-party sources of data, making the integration process very difficult. Information that is found in different sources can be conflicting, overlapping and in unstructured forms, making it difficult to consolidate them. The multiple system consistency is a manual-intensive task that may cause errors and slow down the reporting and decision making. A successful integration is the key to creating a single source of truth of analytics, risk management, and regulatory compliance.

To ensure regulatory compliance, efficient operations, and customer confidence, and to use advanced analytics to assess risks and make decisions, it is crucial that insurers address these issues.

5.2. AI-POWERED ANOMALY DETECTION FOR U.S. DATA SETS

AI-driven anomaly detection is revolutionising U.S. insurance companies' data quality management by analysing unexpected, suspicious, or inconsistent patterns that would have been missed otherwise. Because insurers handle vast amounts of organised and unstructured data, paper-based review methods are slow, resource-intensive, and error-prone. AI algorithms and machine learning help insurers identify claims, policy, and operational data abnormalities in real time, reducing risk and improving decision-making.

- **Claims Data Monitoring:** AI anomaly detection is crucial for claims processing. Monitor claims data. Undiscovered false or dishonest paperwork might cause substantial financial losses. AI models may process historical and real-time claims and discover suspect amounts, submission frequency, and document discrepancies. Automatic highlighting of many claims by the same policyholder or unusually large claim amounts compared to coverage limits are examples. By preventing such abnormalities, insurers can detect fraud, avoid overpayment, and enhance claim accuracy.
- **Policy Records Analysis:** AI anomaly detection is essential for maintaining accurate and consistent policy records. AI helps insurers spot abnormalities in coverage, premiums, beneficiary arrangements, and policy endorsements. This helps identify data inconsistencies and inaccuracies early, decreasing policy mismanagement and regulatory noncompliance. Automated identification reduces manual audits and speeds up corrections and efficiency.
- **Operational Data Surveillance:** AI models can monitor billing cycles, premium collection, and underwriting workflow in addition to claims and policy information. Late premium collections, unexpected underwriting changes, and anomalous billing may suggest systemic problems, procedural flaws, or fraud. Insurers are notified in real time and can take quick corrective action, reducing financial loss and operational risk.

AI models may analyse structured and unstructured data in real time to provide preemptive warnings, such as unsupervised clustering or statistical outlier detection. Early anomaly detection helps insurers reduce losses, improve compliance, and build confidence.

5.3. FUZZY MATCHING AND RECORD CONSOLIDATION

In U.S. insurance companies, data is commonly stored in many systems that are not all linked together, such as old-fashioned systems, cloud services, and external databases. They are often similar in the format in which such systems store information and thus exact matching cannot accurately identify duplicates. Fuzzy matching is an AI-driven method that helps insurers to recognize similar yet different records and, therefore, consolidate them correctly and with better data quality.

❖ Challenges with Exact Matching

Conventional exact matching depends on the same field values which is not usually the case in real insurance data. Common discrepancies include:

- **Names:** Policyholder names vary or abbreviations e.g. Jon Smith and Jonathan Smith cannot be matched by using exact methods.
- **Addresses:** Differences in formatting, abbreviations, or inclusion of unit numbers (e.g., "123 Main St." vs. "123 Main Street, Apt 4B") lead to mismatches.
- **Identifiers:** Duplicate records may be missed because of typographical mistakes or irregular input of policy numbers, account numbers or social security numbers.

These discrepancies lead to inefficiencies in operations, redundancy in processing, and misleading reporting which eventually impact customer service, analytics, and compliance.

❖ Fuzzy Matching Algorithms

Fuzzy matching involves algorithms that help to compute similarity scores between records as opposed to having to match precisely. Levenstein distance, Jaro-Winkler similarity or cosine similarity are some of the techniques that are often obtained to measure the proximity between text strings in names, addresses or any other area. AI-based scoring also makes it more precise by adding background knowledge, semantic associations, and pattern recognition and allows matching records even when there are several deviations.

❖ Record Consolidation

Record consolidation is used to merge similar records into one record of authoritative profile after similar records have been identified. This process ensures that:

- Each policy, claim or policy is uniquely represented in systems.
- Automatic resolution of data inconsistencies leads to better accuracy.
- Analytics, reporting and compliance activities are based on one set of truth and minimizes errors and operational overhead.

❖ Benefits for U.S. Insurers

Fuzzy matching and record consolidation have a variety of benefits to insurance companies:

- **Operational Efficiency:** Lessens manual reconciliation, which saves time and resources.
- **Enhanced Analytics:** Combined files offer the correct information on underwriting, claims, and risk evaluation.

- **Regulatory Compliance:** NAIC, HIPAA, IRS, and SEC reporting are supported by consistent and accurate data.
- **Improved Customer Experience:** Secures information accuracy of policyholders, eliminating delays or mistakes in claims and communication.

U.S. insurers can use the advantages of AI-driven fuzzy matching to guarantee the quality of their data, remove redundancy, and make sound choices throughout the business.

5.4. STANDARDIZATION OF ADDRESS, NAME, AND DATE FIELDS (U.S. POSTAL, SSN, DOB)

More U.S. insurance applications use AI-based data quality and anomaly detection solutions to improve data accuracy, operational risk, and customer happiness. Fraud detection, duplicate policies, and claim rejection prevention are examples. These examples demonstrate how quality, standardised, and aggregated data with AI can transform insurance.

- **Flagging Fraud:** Fraudulent insurance claims cause huge annual losses. AI-based anomaly identification methods can identify suspicious claims data trends using historical and real-time data. To clarify, unexpected claim values, multiple policyholder claims, and timber discretion of supporting papers are under examination. Fraud detection automation will help insurers reduce losses, reduce human review, and comply with regulations. It also expedites valid claims, boosting client confidence.
- **Duplicate Policies:** The presence of duplicate policies might result from several entries in separate systems, inconsistent data formats, or duplicate policy submissions. Replicas can generate operational inefficiencies, false reporting, and regulatory issues. Similar records are

recognised using AI-driven fuzzy matching and record consolidation to integrate policyholder profiles and maintain one source of truth. Duplicates should be recognised and consolidated to reflect one policyholder and one claim, which streamlines billing, reporting, and customer communication.

- **Rejected Claims:** Incomplete, discrepant, or erroneous information in policyholder, beneficiary, or claim records leads to denials. Due to AI-based standardisation, anomaly detection, and data validation, all critical fields (addresses, DOBs, policy information, etc.) will be correct and consistent, reducing claims rejection risk. With better data quality and reliability, insurers can process claims faster, reduce manual involvement, improve customer experience, and comply with NAIC, HIPAA, and other regulations.

AI-driven solutions can automatically identify differences, standardised formats to U.S. Postal Service requirements, sanction SSNs and date of births, and rectify data entry errors, improving data dependability and efficiency.

5.5. U.S. INSURANCE USE CASES: FRAUD FLAGGING, DUPLICATE POLICIES, REJECTED CLAIMS

AI-based data quality solutions enable U.S. insurance businesses efficiently manage large and complex datasets, reduce operational risks, and improve customer satisfaction. Automating claims processing, policy management, and regulatory compliance helps insurers handle real-world data validation, anomaly detection, and record consolidation concerns. Insurance data quality uses of AI include fraud detection, policy duplication, and claim reduction.

- **Fraud Flagging:** Fraudulent claims significantly impact insurance prices. AI-built anomaly detection tools help insurers spot fraudulent claims patterns. Examples include excessive claim values, repeated claims, and documentation errors. Automatic flagging of probable fraud helps insurers detect incidents early, avoid financial advantages, and stay within regulations. Real-time detection speeds up claims processing, paying valid claims quickly.

- **Duplicate Policies:** Caused by data duplication, incorrect formatting, or duplicate entries. AI-powered fuzzy matching and record consolidation algorithms automatically find and consolidate redundant records for one correct policy profile. This reduces operational inefficiencies, overpayment, and misreporting and ensures policyholder data consistency between historical and new systems. Duplication reduction will improve analytics, billing, and customer service for insurers.
- **Rejected Claims:** Inconsistent or incorrect information on policy records or claims forms might lead to denied claims. Standardisation, validation, and anomaly detection using AI help ensure that addresses, birth dates, Social Security numbers, and policy details are correct. AI will reduce claim denials, simplify operations, and improve customer experience by reducing data errors. This also helps insurers meet NAIC, HIPAA, and other rules.

CHAPTER – 6

Machine Learning for Entity Matching

Entity matching Machine learning is used to identify and match comparable records in several datasets, which is crucial to data consolidation and management. Traditional matching systems employ exact rules or manual approaches, which are time-consuming and error-prone, especially for big heterogeneous data sets. Insurance, healthcare, and finance companies receive client information, policy, claims, and transactions from multiple sources with inconsistent spelling, formatting, and other identifiers. Machine learning models may automatically identify records that reflect the same entity despite inconsistencies or errors by acquiring patterns and correlations in data.

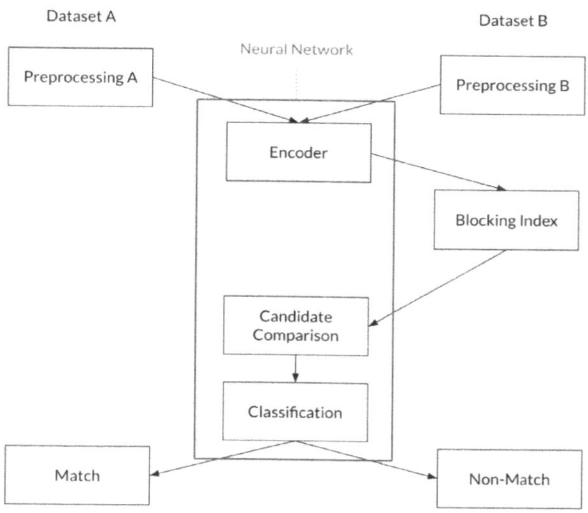

Figure 1: Entity Matching

These models use supervised learning, unsupervised clustering, and probabilistic matching to compare names, addresses, dates, and IDs. Machine learning algorithms can match billing data, link policy history between legacy and new systems, and identify duplicate claims in insurance. In healthcare, ML-based entity matching can align patient records from different hospitals or EHR systems to create a complete medical history. Through historical matches and continual refinement, such algorithms reduce human interaction, improve accuracy, and adapt to data pattern changes.

The operational efficiency of machine learning-based entity matching affects regulatory compliance and data quality. Entity matching is crucial for meeting U.S. compliance standards including HIPAA in medicine, NAIC reporting in insurance, and SEC or IRS data laws in finance. Record duplicates or misalignments can cause inaccurate reporting, regulatory violations, and improper analytics.

6.1. WHAT IS ENTITY RESOLUTION?

Data integration's Entity Resolution (ER) process finds and connects records representing the same real-world entity in multiple datasets. In the U.S. insurance market, customer, policy, claim, agent, and service provider data is often stored in multiple systems, some of which are not connected. Variations of the same data can be stored in different formats, IDs, or naming conventions. John A. Smith may be a policyholder in one system, J. Smith in another, and Jonathan Smith in a third historical claims database. ER is trying to reconcile these disparities into one accurate representation of the entity.

The complexity and diversity of insurance policies has made ER crucial to the U.S. insurance sector. Non-life insurance policies like P and C and health insurance may share client data but differ in areas, identities, and document formats. Agents may use alternative names or addresses and mention partial or unstructured things in policies. ER will integrate these scattered data sets to give insurers a 360-degree view of consumers, policies, and claims.

Risk management and regulation compliance depend on ER. Proper entity linking helps insurers meet NAIC, HIPAA, SEC, and IRS reporting requirements, reducing fines. The ER helps detect fraud by revealing trends that may be hidden in other systems, such as false claims from the same person or address with minor service identifier changes. It helps insurers segment, price, and underwrite customers more accurately through analytics and business intelligence.

Based on earlier data analysis, AI and machine learning can identify duplicate or related records in unstructured, partial, or inconsistent data in modern ER approaches. Fuzzy matching, probabilistic linkage models, and NLP are used to find similarities in names, addresses, dates, and other crucial variables.

6.2. SUPERVISED VS. UNSUPERVISED LEARNING TECHNIQUES

In the U.S. insurance industry, entity resolution (ER) may make use of both supervised and unsupervised machine learning methods based on the labelled data at hand, the complexity of the data and operational demands. These methods allow the insurers to segment the records of numerous systems accurately and then correlate them with each other, despite the inconsistency, incompleteness, and unstructured nature of the data.

❖ Supervised Learning for Entity Resolution

Supervised learning is based on labelled datasets indicating the pairs of records that are associated with the same entity (labeled match) or not. Such labelled examples may be known a priori pairs of policyholder records, claims or profiles of agents in the case of insurance. These features are fed into machine learning algorithms like logistic regression, random forests, gradient boosting, or neural networks to learn patterns that are used to identify a match.

Supervised ER is very precise and trustworthy in situations where adequate labelled data is available because it can distinguish sophisticated relationships and fine changes amid records. Nevertheless, the accuracy will need ongoing retraining due to the fact that insurance datasets change as time goes on with new policies, claims and customer interactions. Besides, labelling of data may be hectic and expensive, especially when dealing with big-scale insurance processes.

❖ Unsupervised Learning for Entity Resolution

Unsupervised learning does not use labelled data, but instead uses similarity measures, clustering algorithms or probabilistic models to determine records that probably represent the same entity. Common techniques include:

- **Hierarchical clustering:** Groups similar records in a tree-like structure based on defined similarity metrics.
- **K-means clustering:** Partitions records into clusters based on similarity scores.
- **Probabilistic record linkage:** Estimates the likelihood that two records represent the same entity using statistical models.

Unsupervised techniques are also well-suited to large insurance data sets in which labelled data is either scarce or expensive to access. They are able to identify the duplicates, connect customer profiles and relationships across policies, claims, and agents without a lot of manual intervention.

6.3. FEATURE ENGINEERING FOR MATCHING U.S. INSURANCE RECORDS

Entity resolution (ER) includes an important step of feature engineering, turning raw insurance data into meaningful, structured variables that machine learning models can then utilize to find and match records in the correct way. The U.S. insurance industry is associated with heterogeneous data, which is distributed over various systems and in unstructured formats, and that is why the feature engineering is needed to extract the similarities and connections between the entities. Well-designed features enhance the model accuracy, decrease false positives and false negatives, and augment interpretability.

❖ Personal Identifiers

Personal identifiers are among the most important features for matching records across insurance datasets. Key identifiers include:

- **Names:** Full names, first and last names, initials, and variations.
- **Addresses:** Street addresses, apartment numbers, cities, ZIP codes, and state abbreviations.
- **Dates of Birth (DOB):** Standardized formats are critical to avoid mismatches.
- **Social Security Numbers (SSNs):** Unique identifiers that, when accurate, provide strong matching signals.

In these areas, advanced methods, including fuzzy string matching, phonetic encoding (e.g., Soundex), and tokenization, are frequently used to deal with spelling variations, abbreviations, or typographical errors.

❖ Policy Details

Policy features are crucial in the connection between policyholder records and coverage and the related claims. Key policy characteristics are as follows:

- Policy numbers and identifiers

- Coverage types and levels
- Effective and expiration dates
- Riders, add-ons, and policy endorsements

Machine learning models are used to determine records corresponding to the same policy or similar policies in different systems, despite differences in identifiers or description.

❖ **Claims Attributes**

Claims information offers rich entity resolution opportunities especially on connecting claimants, policies and related agents. Key features include:

- Claim IDs and reference numbers
- Submission dates and timestamps
- Claim amounts and payout history
- Claim status (approved, pending, rejected)

Text-based fields, like description of a claim, or attached documents, can need NLP methods of extracting features, like embeddings, tokenization, and semantic similarity.

❖ **Agent and Provider Information**

Linking agents, brokers, and providers to policies and claims is another critical task. Features in this category include:

- Agent or provider IDs
- Names, contact details, and addresses
- Licenses, certifications, and state registrations
- Affiliated insurance companies or networks

In addition to the policyholder and claims information, these features turn useful to the insurers, as they are able to see relationships throughout the insurance ecosystem to more easily assess risk, detect fraud, and support operational controls.

Advanced feature engineering can also use text similarity, phonetic encodings, tokenization, and semantic encodings, particularly with unstructured data such as claims notes or emails. Well-engineered features enhance accuracy in matching, decrease false positives/negatives, and the model interpretability.

6.4. USING ML TO LINK POLICIES, CUSTOMERS, AGENTS IN THE U.S. MARKET

Machine learning (ML) is a key to bridging discrepancies in records between policies, customers, and agents of the insurance industry in the United States. Insurers tend to deal with vast amount of fragmented information in old systems, third-party platforms and across different product lines. ML algorithms have the ability to process both structured and unstructured data to discover relationships automatically, delivering a single perspective of entities and improving operational effectiveness, risk management and compliance.

- **Customer-to-Policy Matching:** ML models have the capability to recognize up to and including all those policies that a particular individual has even in the event of name, address or any other identifying attributes being different across systems. The fuzzy matching, probabilistic linkage, and NLP-based similarity scoring are examples of techniques that enable models to identify the slight discrepancies and guarantee correct connections. It allows an insurer to unify the customer records, minimize the duplication, and have a single source of truth that is needed to conduct portfolio analysis, personalized marketing, and claims management.
- **Policy-to-Agent Linking:** Properly linking policies to responsible agents is essential in monitoring commissions,

sales performance and regulatory reporting requirements. ML algorithms are capable of mapping policies to agents automatically using an identifier, historical transaction data, or cross-referenced records. Such connectivity also enables the insurers to track the conduct of the agents, identify patterns that are abnormal and also to bring about accountability with the state-level regulations. Automation of these connections aids the insurers in cutting their manual workload and enhancing the accuracy of operational reporting and agent accountability.

- **Cross-Policyholder Connections:** Machine learning is capable of establishing policyholder relations as well: shared address, family relations, business connections. It is significant to detect these links to determine the exposure of risks, possible fraud, and enhance underwriting decisions. As an example, several policies submitted in the same address but with minor differences in the name might point to the possibility of fraud or co-ordinated claims. ML-based insights allow insurers to proactively investigate those cases, reducing the losses and improving the security of the entire portfolio.

The ML-based connections lead to better risk assessment, better portfolio management, better fraud detection, and better customer service, with fragmented information consolidated and actionable insights provided.

6.5. MERGING STRUCTURED AND UNSTRUCTURED DATA (E.G., CLAIMS NOTES, PDFS, EHRS)

U.S. insurance industry datasets are usually a combination of structured and unstructured data that each holds value information that is important in operations, compliance, and decisions. Structured data consists of structured fields that are usually policy numbers, premium, claim IDs, coverage type, and beneficiary information and are normally found in relational databases or enterprise resource planning. Unstructured data, in their turn, include text-heavy or media-rich content, such as claim stories, emails, PDFs, scanned documents, and electronic health records (EHRs).

❖ Challenges of Merging Structured and Unstructured Data

Merging structured and unstructured data poses several challenges:

- **Format Diversity:** Structure Data Structured data is organized and standardized, whereas unstructured data may include free text, images, or scanned forms with many different forms.
- **Data Extraction Complexity:** Relevant data, e.g. medical diagnoses within EHRs or policy terms within PDFs, have to be mined and standardized to be incorporated.
- **Legacy System Constraints:** Older insurance systems might not be able to store or process unstructured data effectively to form silos.
- **Consistency and Accuracy:** Structuring the unstructured sources of fields in correlation with structured records demands sophisticated methods to prevent duplication and misclassification.

❖ AI and NLP Solutions

Current AIs and Natural Language Processing (NLP) systems alleviate these issues by facilitating automatic data mining and meaning interpretation of non-structured data. For example:

- **Claim Narratives:** NLP algorithms are able to extract numbers of claims, dates, or cause-of-loss information on free-text descriptions.

- **Medical Data from EHRs:** Model machine learning can identify diagnoses, treatments, and identifiers of patients and match them to policyholder records to use in health insurance claims.
- **PDFs and Scanned Documents:** OCR and AI can be used together to transform images into processed text to be analyzed and incorporated.

These tools enable insurers to connect extracted data with structured records and, therefore, provide complete entity resolution and avoids an absence between legacy and modern systems.

❖ Business Applications

Merging structured and unstructured data provides multiple benefits:

- **Fraud Detection:** Bringing all information together can help to detect anomalies or duplicate claims that might be missed otherwise.
- **Claims Adjudication:** Automated date extraction makes it fast and less prone to errors which enhances customer satisfaction.
- **Analytics and Insights:** Combined datasets facilitates predictive modelling, risk analysis, and optimization of operation.
- **Regulatory Compliance:** Precise and consolidated information is used to satisfy reporting needs of NAIC, HIPAA, SEC and IRS requirements.

U.S. insurers are able to combine both structured and unstructured data to gain a 360-degree picture of policyholders, policies, claims, and agents to improve decision-making, operational efficiency, and competitive advantage.

The U.S insurance industry has a long history of entity resolution where the two categories of data are merged to form a complete picture. NLP (Natural Language Processing) and AI systems are able to find the fields of interest in unstructured data, including narratives of claims, diagnosis reports, or messages to customers, and match them to records. It provides the ability to detect frauds accurately, adjudicate claims, and analytics, filling the information gaps between legacy databases and new data repositories.

CHAPTER – 7

Intelligent ETL And Workflow Automation

Artificial Intelligence (AI) in ETL and process automation is altering the US insurance sector by removing inefficiencies. Ad-hoc flexible solutions are replaced with rigorous, rule-based ETL pipelines that automate schema mapping, anomaly detection, predictive error replies, and dynamic rule transformation. This simplifies integration of heterogeneous data like policyholder records, medical reports, telematics, and IoT. In addition, real-time ETL extracts, transforms, and loads data immediately after creation, improving claim accuracy and settlement time.

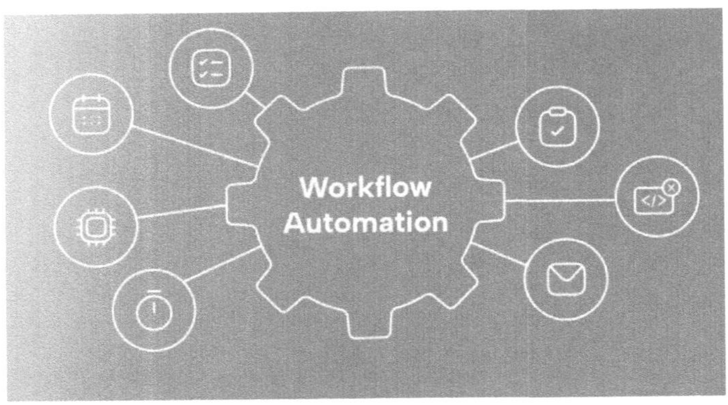

Figure 1: Workflow Automation

ETL and AI-based process automation revolutionized how insurance companies do business and interact with clients. Intelligent scheduling sets priorities based on urgency, risk, and regulation and dynamically allocates resources to avoid bottlenecks. Workload forecasting anticipates changes in workloads to ensure service continuity during natural disasters and claims spikes. Workflow recommender systems can guide underwriters, claim handlers, and agents along optimal decision paths, suggesting next-best actions and highlighting process inefficiencies. This self-learning system improves procedures and gives employees of different skills individual recommendations. Stable, productive, and adaptable operations boost staff productivity and customer pleasure.

Additionally, event-driven IoT pipelines make insurance real-time responsive. Telematics, smart home sensors, and wearable continuous signals can automate claim initiation, generate underwriting warning signals, and adjust rates to risk exposure changes. A telematics-reported crash can start a claim, while abnormal driving or health changes can need underwriting re-evaluation. Changing premium structures from non-dynamic, annualized models to behavior-based and usage-based pricing brings justice, transparency, and customer interaction.

7.1. AI-AUGMENTED ETL PIPELINE ARCHITECTURE

Conventional ETL (Extract, Transform, Load) solutions are rule-based and inflexible, which is why they are less efficient with large and heterogeneous semi-structured data that are prevalent in the U.S. insurance industry, including policyholder records, medical reports, call transcripts, telematics on vehicles, and IoT data on smart devices. With AI in ETL, these pipelines are smarter, more adaptive and more resilient.

1. **Automated Schema Mapping:** AI models may be trained to learn the structure and semantics of data in multiple sources (databases, APIs, third-party platforms, cloud storage) and automatically make them conform to a common schema. As an example, the customer demographics stored in various forms in policy management and claims systems can be seamlessly reconciled.

2. **Fraud and error Detection:** Machine learning algorithms can scan incoming claims, transactions or sensor data continuously to identify anomalies that do not match the normal pattern. This will allow insurers to voluntarily deter fraudulent claims, identify input errors, and detect suspicious activity so that the cost is saved and trust is enhanced.
3. **Dynamic Transformation Rules:** Machine learning can optimize and even re-write transformation logic dynamically to adapt to the new forms of data or to changing regulatory demands. An example of this is when a new compliance rule alters the manner in which the claims information is to be reported, the system can make the adjustments without having to undergo an extensive re-coding process.
4. **Predictive Error Handling:** AI-based ETL is able to make predictions about what should be fixed rather than fail at mismatches or omit fields, using its prior knowledge and historical evidence. This saves time, enhances the accuracy of data and guarantees high quality of inputs to analytics and reporting systems.

The outcome is a faster, scalable and responsive pipeline to the dynamism of the U.S insurance environment. It facilitates regulatory adherence (e.g. HIPAA in health insurance, NAIC data formats), streamlines operations, lessens losses due to fraud, and ultimately improves decision-making in underwriting, claims and customer service departments.

7.2. INTELLIGENT SCHEDULING AND DATA PRIORITIZATION IN U.S. INSURANCE FIRMS

Insurance companies have a huge number of concurrent processes to execute, such as paying claims and renewing the policies but also dealing with the interactions of the customers; responding to regulatory reporting requirements. Conventional scheduling usually operates by fixed rules or batch scheduling, resulting in bottlenecks, misses in deadlines and customer dissatisfaction.

1. **Urgency and Importance:** AI systems have the ability to prioritize tasks based upon contextual elements including claim size, customer profile, and possible risk. As an illustration, when a high-value claim comes across a long-term corporate client, it will be automatically prioritized over regular updates, and critical cases are addressed in time.
2. **Dynamic Resource Allocation:** AI models do not allocate work to fixed teams or amount of server capacity, but observe real-time demand and distribute resources (human adjusters, customer agents or computational power) to the most demanded areas. This saves time wastage during settlement of claims and cuts down efficiency in operations.
3. **Compliance-Based Scheduling:** The U.S. presence of insurance companies has to adhere to strict deadlines as part of regulations like NAIC (National Association of Insurance Commissioners) reporting or HIPAA regarding health-related claims. The AI systems are automatically able to recognize the tasks, which have compliance-related deadlines, and push them to the top of the queue to decrease the possibility of fines and legal liability.
4. **Predictive Workload Forecasting:** AI predicts rises in workloads by examining past data and seasonal trends and other external factors (such as natural disasters leading to peaks in claim counts). This allows companies to anticipate in advance the availability of workforce, modify the shift

time, or its processing power in the system to deal with spikes with ease.

This smart prioritization will result in more claims being handled more quickly, more consistently fulfilling compliance obligations, and more efficiently addressing customer service requests. Consequently, insurers are in a position to save on the time required to settle a claim, increase their compliance with regulations, and overall customer satisfaction without increasing operation expenses.

7.3. AI FOR WORKFLOW RECOMMENDER SYSTEMS

AI-supported recommender systems guide insurance professionals to the most efficient decision-making procedures. Claim handlers, underwriters, and customer service agents must use consistent judgement when verifying documents, reviewing eligibility, or escalating cases. From historical data and good results, AI may recommend the next best action in each process phase. It can propose that an underwriter request more documentation for complicated health claims or auto-approve low-risk, low-value claims. This reduces errors and inter-agent variability and speeds up task completion.

In addition to quick decision-making, AI recommenders evaluate organisational data to optimise processes. They identify inefficiencies like unnecessary approval steps and bottlenecks and offer workflow improvements. This improves process adaptation and optimisation over time. To tailor workflows to car, health, property, and life insurance claims, the system can tailor its recommendations. In auto accident claims, visual evidence analysis may be prioritized, but in health insurance claims, medical coding standards may be.

Because individuals and teams vary in strength, workload, and responsibility, workflow recommenders might be agent or department-specific. The system can customize recommendations to orient new hires through standardised processes and provide more advanced and efficient advice to experienced professionals. Personalization reduces decision fatigue, improves performance, and standardizes business and regulatory compliance. This gives insurers a faster claims turnaround, happier employees, and a better customer experience while maintaining a robust, compliant, and successful operating landscape.

7.4. REAL-TIME ETL IN CLAIMS PROCESSING

In the insurance industry, claims processing is time- and pressure-sensitive since it affects client happiness, retention, and trust. Batch-based ETL systems delay data extraction, transformation, and loading. Real-time ETLs can extract data from mobile claim submission apps, hospital information systems, police reports, repair shop invoices, and IoT sensors in connected cars or smart devices. Capturing and processing claims data in real time provides a continuous, real-time decision-making basis.

Data are extracted and converted on-the-fly to standardised, unstructured data insurance systems can interpret. Claims data, such as medical records, police reports, and IoT sensor data, might be unstructured or semi-structured, requiring real-time processing. AI-enabled ETL solutions can scrape, clean, and normalise data in real time without human intervention, maintaining consistency and accuracy. This organised information is delivered directly into decision-support engines, where autonomous algorithms, machine learning, and predictive analytics analyse the assertion, check qualifications, and assess authenticity in near real time.

Proactive fraud prevention and transparency are extra benefits of real-time ETL claim processing. Advanced anomaly detection models can detect suspect patterns in claims like duplicates, misaligned timelines, and exaggerated costs, preventing fraud before settlement. Reduce settlement time, reduce fraudulent payouts, and ensure an auditable and transparent claims process with real-time ETL to boost operational efficiency, customer confidence, and technology-driven insurance.

7.5. EVENT-DRIVEN PIPELINES: IOT DATA AND UNDERWRITING ALERTS

IoT sensors like telematics systems on cars, smart home sensors, and wearable health watches generate high-frequency streams of data that have a lot of potential to change the insurance industry underwriting and claims management. Conversely, purpose-built event driven pipelines have been developed to receive, process, and act on IoT signals in real time to help insurers shift to being reactive to decisions, rather than proactive to those decisions, thus enhancing risk management, operational effectiveness, and customer satisfaction.

- **Real-time processing of IoT signals:** Event-driven architecture: Event-driven architecture enables the insurers to react in real-time to the IoT events. An example is; in cases where telematics sensors capture a vehicle-collision a claim can be automatically triggered without involving the manual declaration of the policy-holder. This high level of responsiveness in real-time not only speeds up the process of claims settlement but also generates customer trust and loyalty by reducing delays in high-stress situations.
- **Creating underwriting signals:** In addition to claims, event-driven pipelines facilitate an ongoing risk check throughout the policy lifecycle. They can also ensure that the insurers come up with dynamic rules that alert underwriting whenever the key risk factors vary. Such

alerts enable insurers to revisit and re-price risk exposure on an ongoing basis to facilitate more precise underwriting decision-making and mitigate the possible losses.

- **Premium adjustment:** Active pipelines are also suitable to individualized and adaptive pricing models. In lieu of fixed, annual premium designs, insurers can use IoT-enabled behavioral data to provide usage-based or performance-based pricing. This change toward real-time, data-driven premium adjustments provides fairness, transparent and better alignment of the actual exposure to risk and price, and in the long-run, customer engagement and encouraging of positive behavior.

Essentially, event-based IoT data pipelines redefine insurance value chain by changing the processes into dynamic and responsive systems. They do not only simplify claims management processes and optimize underwriting operations but also pave the way to new insurance products, risk prevention measures, and enhanced connections with customers in a data-driven environment.

PART-III

IMPLEMENTING AI-DRIVEN TRANSFORMATION

CHAPTER – 8

Use Cases in Life And P&C Insurance

AI is modernizing U.S. life insurance and P&C operations by improving policy control, underwriting, claims, and regulatory compliance. AI-powered ETL technologies automate data extraction, cleansing, and mapping to migrate old life insurance policies, reducing human error, operational risks, and regulatory compliance. AI-powered underwriting models incorporate medical history and wearable data to improve risk assessment, pricing, and adverse selection. Customer 360 programs use structured and unstructured data across multiple touchpoints to provide targeted policy recommendations, detect fraud, and interact proactively, building customer trust and retention.

Figure 1: P&C Insurance

AI is changing NAIC's claims handling, product integration, and regulatory reporting in the U.S. P&C business. Natural Language Processing (NLP), computer vision, and IoT data improve claims processing, damages assessment, fraud detection, and automated settlement approvals, reducing cycle times and loss adjustment costs.

In the U.S., AI in insurance reduces project risk, cost, and time. AI decreases operational and strategic risk by monitoring data, predicting problems, and simulating. Real-time compliance tracking and audit-ready reports from AI provide regulatory certainty, and accelerated and automated workflows improve customer experience by processing claims faster and issuing policies with hyper-personalized interactions for operational efficiency, customer satisfaction, and competitive advantage.

8.1. LIFE INSURANCE: POLICY MIGRATION, UNDERWRITING RISK MODELING, CUSTOMER 360

U.S. life insurance is being transformed by heritage modernisation, sophisticated underwriting, and customer-centricity. AI-enabled ETL software automatically maps the schema, purifies and verifies decades of fragmented data, and ensures regulatory compliance, speeding policy migration from older to digital systems. This eliminates human work, reduces operational risks, and accelerates insurers' digital transformation. Underwriting risk modelling is moving beyond actuarial processes to AI-based processes that combine medical and genetic data, wearables, and more to improve prediction, pricing, risk categorisation, and minimise adverse selection.

Customer 360 uses structured and unstructured data from many touchpoints to develop a complete policyholder profile. AI can combine demographics, payment and claims history, email insights, chatbot interactions, and speech transcripts into an actionable view. This whole-picture strategy improves retention and trust through customised policy advice, fraud detection, and proactive client interaction. All these advancements indicate a shift towards data-driven, adaptive, and customer-centric insurance.

- ***Policy Migration***

Life insurance companies in the United States that still use legacy policy administration systems tend to have decades of historical information stored in fragmented, outdated formats and therefore modernization is complex and risky. The process of moving these policies to the more sophisticated digital platforms entails cautious procedures of extraction, cleansing, mapping, and verifying large amounts of information pertaining to policyholders and policies. AI-based ETL applications simplify this task by automating schema mapping, identifying anomalies or data inconsistencies and facilitating platform-to-platform integration. This minimizes human mistakes, decreases downtime in the transition process, and assists insurers in achieving compliance and regulatory requirements contributing to accelerating the digital transformation process.

- ***Underwriting Risk Modeling***

The use of AI in risk modeling is becoming the new direction of life insurance underwriting that is no longer based on traditional actuarial methods. Insurers can gain a better understanding of mortality and morbidity risks by incorporating a wide range of information, including electronic medical history, laboratory findings, prescription history, understanding of genetic testing, and even lifestyle indicators (via wearables). Machine learning algorithms help to make predictions with greater precision, identify latent correlations and undergo continuous refinement on the basis of additional data. The resultant effect of this is better classification of risks, better pricing strategies, less adverse selection and competitive advantage in the market.

- ***Customer 360***

Customer 360 programs seek to create an integrated, comprehensive characterization of every policyholder by gathering information in various customer interactions, including policy apps and call center logs, plus claims records and online interaction tools. AI technologies allow combining the structured data (e.g., demographic information, a history of payments) and the unstructured ones (e.g., emails, chatbot interactions, voice recordings). The resultant single customer view enables the insurers to provide personalized policy recommendation, improve customer service, enhance customer retention strategy, and detect potentially fraudulent activities in the real time. Using Customer 360, insurers will be able to shift to more customer-centric, proactive, and trust-based business models.

8.2. P&C INSURANCE: CLAIMS MANAGEMENT, PRODUCT INTEGRATION, NAIC REGULATORY REPORTING

AI is transforming the U.S. Property and casualty insurance P&C industry in the areas of claims management, product integration, and regulation reporting. Traditionally manual and error-prone claims processing now takes advantage of AI-based solutions, such as NLP, to identify important information in unstructured data, IoT and telematics to support real-time incident proofs, and computer vision to assess damage, estimate costs, and identify frauds, allowing faster, more precise, and automatic claim settlements. Also, AI simplifies NAIC regulatory reporting by automating the compilation of data, mapping to the accepted templates, identifying inconsistencies, and conforming to the evolving regulations, which would consume less manual work and improve regulatory compliance and enable the teams to concentrate on proactive risk management.

- ***Claims Management***

Claims management in the U.S. Property and Casualty (P&C) insurance industry is experiencing a major change with the automation of ways of handling claims, mediated by AI. Historically, claims processing has been a manual intensive and time-consuming process, which tends to be full of error and delays. Now, AI technologies like Natural Language Processing (NLP) are used to automatically derive crucial information out of unstructured sources of data, such as incident reports, customer statements and third-party documentation. Computer vision models also extend the assessment features, verifying the uploaded photos and videos to know the magnitude of damages, estimate repairs and identify anomalies that may be a sign of fraud, including staged crashes or doctored images. These AI-driven insights are inputted into event workflows, which prioritize work based on claims triage, assigning the proper adjusters and, in certain instances, generating an automated settlement approval.

- ***Product Integration***

To improve customer retention and increase the chances of cross-selling, insurers in the highly competitive U.S. P&C market often bundle their products such as auto, home, renters, and flood insurance together to maximize their use. ETL (Extract, Transform, Load) systems that use AI are vital in unifying and harmonizing data between these product lines of diversity. With these systems, overlapping coverages are automatically reconciled, underwriting rules are standardized and disparate policy information is maintained. Insurers can have a smooth and harmonized customer journey by putting such information together in a single platform, including integrated billing, cross-policy discounts, and personalized products recommendations based on customer usage and risk profiles.

- ***NAIC Regulatory Reporting***

U.S. P&C insurers are also subject to tough reporting standards established by the National Association of Insurance Commissioners (NAIC), including the solvency monitoring, the adequacy of risk-based capital, market conduct and consumer protection. Addressing these regulatory requirements requires consolidation and control of large volumes of data between many internal and external systems. This is complicated by reporting solutions powered by AI that automatize it by mapping insurer data to NAIC-approved templates, finding inconsistencies or anomalies before submission, and dynamically responding to changes in state-level regulations. The outcome is that manual work can be reduced, reporting mistakes can be avoided, and the transparency can be facilitated, and it can all assist insurers in evading regulatory fines and reputational damage.

8.3. END-TO-END MIGRATION CASE STUDY: AI FROM DISCOVERY TO CUTOVER IN A U.S. INSURER

The policy migration procedure at a major U.S. life insurance firm was transformed by AI, making it faster and more accurate. The discovery stage of the transfer involved using AI-based analytics tools to scan existing systems to learn about the sophisticated data model, metadata format, and ETL operations. This allowed correct migration step planning and foresaw potential disputes and high-risk regions that needed project team attention, reducing uncertainty early on.

Machine learning algorithms automatically identified duplicates, missing values, inconsistent codes, and formatting irregularities in millions of policyholder records in the second step, data quality and cleansing. The AI found and suggested corrections to errors and usually fixed them and preserved sterile audit records instead of manually checking the data. This ensured high-quality data before entering the target system, reduced downstream error, and improved regulatory compliance. This allowed insurers to achieve precision that would have been nearly unachievable in manual methods, laying the groundwork for the next phase of transformation.

AI created target-platform-specific transformation logic during transformation and testing, boosting migration. Parallel tests were undertaken to match modified data to source records and assure accuracy. To facilitate input and modification, the system automatically identified, classified, and rectified differences. This AI solution reduced manual reconciliation and testing and uniformly applied rules to millions of policy documents without affecting regulatory compliance or business continuity.

8.4. HOW AI REDUCES PROJECT RISK, COST, AND TIME IN U.S. IMPLEMENTATIONS

In U.S. insurance projects, AI is used to improve risk management, efficiency, and customer outcomes, among others, by actively detecting anomaly, anticipating possible failures, and simulating scenarios to reduce operational and strategic risks. It saves time as it automates the complex tasks such as schema mapping, transformation logic, and testing, it requires fewer resources and no mistakes or rework. All of these capabilities enhance the reliability of operations and provide more personalized services in a shorter time, enhancing customer satisfaction, retention, and competitive advantage.

- **Risk Reduction:** AI technologies are very instrumental in reducing the project risks in the U.S. insurance implementations. Through constant data and workflow observation, AI will be able to identify anomalies and discrepancies early in the process of the migration or transformation, before they become major problems. Predictive models also determine the potential of possible migration failures so that the project teams can take measures to change strategies in advance. Second, AI-based simulations enable stakeholders to experiment with different situations and predict the future, which will give a controlled setting to predict difficult situations and design mitigation strategies and thus reduce operational and strategic risks.

- **Cost Efficiency:** AI implementation will greatly cut costs of projects as a number of resource-consuming tasks are automated. The AI systems are capable of automatic schema mapping, creation of transformation logic and engage in large-scale testing processes that would otherwise have been handled by highly skilled and high-cost consultants. This automation does not just reduce the direct cost of human resource, but it is also less likely to make expensive errors, rework and delays.
- **Time Savings:** AI helps to scale up several stages of insurance operations, such as data finding, data migration, and regulatory audit. Automating repetitive and high-volume tasks, AI reduces project timeframes dramatically, turning initiatives, which would otherwise take years to accomplish, into projects that can be accomplished in months. Further efficiency and time-to-value Project teams can invest more effort into strategic decision-making with faster data processing, intelligent validation, and automated reporting.
- **Regulatory Assurance:** There are strict state and federal regulations of U.S. insurance projects. AI makes this compliance possible by automatically checking processes against regulatory needs, raising alerts when there is a potential non-compliance issue in real time, and creating audit-ready reports. This ongoing control over compliance minimizes the possibility of regulatory fines and facilitates the smooth compliance with the legal norms, increasing the reliability of operations and the trustworthiness of the organization.

- **Customer Impact:** AI implementation has a positive impact on customer experience. Faster data migrations and automated workflows will allow accomplishing the faster claims processing, issuing policies timely and in the most personalized way. These enhancements do not only raise customer satisfaction; it also enhances retention and loyalty making the insurers have a competitive advantage in a competitive market that is growing competitive.

CHAPTER – 9

Cross-Industry Perspectives in The U.S.

AI is automating operational data, workflow, and regulatory compliance in U.S. financial, government, and healthcare services, revolutionizing them. AI automates loan origination, including unstructured and structured data extraction and normalization, and predictive models identify high-risk applications and creditworthiness, speeding loan approvals and reducing manual errors. Compliance with SEC and FDIC laws and reduced penalties and reputational risks are improved by AI-driven financial data aggregation, validation, and reporting. Government The IRS uses AI to automate data extraction, reconciliation, anomaly detection, and predictive auditing to improve compliance, resource allocation, and taxpayer trust. Healthcare AI enables EHR interoperability, HIPAA claims scrubbing, routine process automation, regulatory compliance, and faster and more accurate patient and provider services.

Critical learning from cross-industry applications can be applied to U.S. insurance. Data integration and interoperability in banks, government, and healthcare allows insurers to integrate structured policy records, unstructured claims documents, and IoT feeds into AI-centric pipelines for real-time insights, risk analysis, and customized customer experiences. Toddler compliance teams may use SEC / FDIC and HIPAA enforcement automation to manage state and federal insurance rules, provide audit-ready data, and proactively identify violations to focus on strategic efforts. Events-driven real-time architectures enable dynamic pricing, internet-of-things underwriting, and risk warning systems that allow insurers to react to market conditions. AI can assist U.S. insurance improve operational efficiency, customer satisfaction, manual burden, regulatory and fraud compliance, and provide a more data-driven, adaptable, and competitive sector.

9.1. FINANCIAL SERVICES: LOAN ORIGINATION, SEC/FDIC COMPLIANCE, AML MONITORING

The U.S. financial industry is undergoing a revolution in terms of loans such as the AI that automated the data processing, regulatory compliance, and anti-money laundering (AML) monitoring processes by automating data processing, risk assessment, and reporting. In the loan origination process, predictive models, AIs yank data out of applications and credit reports and condition documents, and workflow automation normalizes the data and analyzes creditworthiness, as well as identifies high-risk cases, speeding up the process and minimizing the number of errors made by humans. Machine learning is more effective in identifying suspicious patterns of transactions, reduces false positives and simplifies the investigation process in AML monitoring, allowing compliance teams to prioritize authentic high-risk activity and enhance overall operational efficiency.

- ***Loan Origination***

Fintech companies, banks and credit unions are increasingly using AI-based ETL and workflow automation to automate the process of loan origination. The AI systems identify and process automatic data information in application forms that are structured or unstructured and supporting documents that are unstructured and credit bureau reports, automatically extracting and normalizing information. High-tech predictive systems are used to evaluate creditworthiness and predict the possibility of default so that the institution can flag high-risk applications early. Through its automation of such functions, AI saves both underwriting effort (manual) and human error and decreases the total time to get approval.

- ***SEC/FDIC Compliance***

The United States financial institutions must follow the strict rules that are imposed by the Federal Deposit Insurance Corporation (FDIC) and the Securities and Exchange Commission (SEC). Compliance is sustained reporting, risk monitoring and audit preparedness. AI solutions automate aggregation of vast amounts of data at the same time, including efforts of various internal and external sources, and verify the correctness of financial records, and create the full scope of regulatory reports in real-time. This automation ensures that reporting mistakes are reduced, deadlines are always met and institutions are in line with the changing regulatory requirements, therefore reducing the risk of fines and the negative publicity.

- ***AML (Anti-Money Laundering) Monitoring***

Machine learning and artificial intelligence models facilitate the detection of financial transfer in case of money laundering. With this, AI is able to detect abnormalities in transactions by comparing the transactional history of various accounts and reporting this as suspicious behavior which can be an indication of fraud. This not only fulfills the requirements of the U.S. Anti-Money Laundering laws, but also enhances business efficiency as the compliance teams can concentrate on real high-risk cases and do not need to be overwhelmed with inaccurate alarms.

9.2. HEALTHCARE: EHR INTEROPERABILITY, HIPAA COMPLIANCE, CMS CLAIMS SCRUBBING

AI is reshaping the work of the U.S. government by automating the data processing, workflow, and service delivery among the agencies. Using AI-based ETL systems at the IRS processes tax filings, identifies irregularities, and focuses on high-risk audits, promoting compliance and revenue protection. DMV services make use of AI to check identities, check fraud, and simplify processing of vehicles and licenses, which saves time and administrative resources. In the sphere of citizen services, AI combines data of various kinds to speed up the benefits and Social Security applications, as well as public health programs, enhance their accuracy, efficiency, transparency, and public satisfaction.

- **IRS Data Transformation**

Internal Revenue Service (IRS) is an agency that receives a huge number of tax compliance, payments, and other records annually. Handling this volume and complexity of data manually is time-consuming, but also subject to errors and inconsistency. Now AI and state-of-the-art ETL (Extract, Transform, Load) applications are more than ever critical in converting this data into a usable and accurate form. AI-supported applications automate tax returns ingestion and processing, link payments on many accounts, and detect anomalies that might indicate fraud or discrepancies, in millions of individual and corporate records. Moreover, predictive modeling and machine learning algorithms allow the IRS to identify high-risk filings, focus on investigations and maximize auditing resource allocations.

- **DMV Services**

The activities of the Department of Motor Vehicles (DMV), in particular, the issuance of driver licenses, the registration of vehicles, and identity verification are being more and more automated with the help of AI. AI systems are capable of automatically recognizing duplicates or other fraudulent entries, checking the validity of the identity and other submitted documents, and signaling inconsistencies in real time. This automation saves administration overheads on DMV personnel and it drastically shortens wait times at the service centers. With AI and intelligent workflow management, DMV agencies can offer citizens a more trustworthy and usable experience and achieve a high level of regulatory compliance and record integrity.

- **Citizen Services**

In federal, state and local government agencies, AI-based data integration and workflow automation are remaking the provision of services by the government. To respond more quickly and accurately to the requests made by citizens, systems are now combining and analyzing data across various sources- such as employment records, Social Security databases, and public health registries. As an example, AI can be used to easily handle unemployment benefits claims, Social Security applications, and even the administration of the public health programs, and these applications would be administered and rendered in a timely and accurate manner. Enhancing reliability of the offered services, their efficiency and transparency, AI enhances the trust in the government and satisfaction among citizens and enables the governmental bodies to concentrate on proactive management of the programs and making proper decisions.

9.3. GOVERNMENT: DATA TRANSFORMATION FOR IRS, DMV, AND CITIZEN SERVICES

The U.S. government is improving its operations through the use of AI to automate data management and the workflow processes, as well as delivery of services to the populace. In the IRS, AI-based ETL and predictive analytics are used to improve efficiency and compliance, streamline tax data processing, identify anomalies, and rank high-risk audits. In the federal, state, and local agencies, services, including unemployment benefits, Social Security, and public health programs, use AI to integrate and analyze data and reduce errors, deliver faster responses, and enhance transparency, efficiency, and customer satisfaction.

- **IRS Data Transformation:** The internal Revenue service (IRS) utilizes a large volume of information, comprising tax returns, payment history, and audit trail to millions of taxpayers in the United States. Intelligent AI and powerful ETL applications can provide much better efficiency and accuracy of these procedures. Such systems not only automate the extraction, transformation and reconciliation of tax information, but also identify anomalies and possible fraud. AI can shorten the duration of auditing processes, minimize the number of human errors, and guarantee that tax processes in the U.S are performed in a timely fashion.
- **DMV Services:** AI-powered automation is of immense benefit to DMV operations, which include issuing licenses, registering vehicles, and verifying an individual. Algorithms based on AI can identify duplicates, establish a true identity of documents and indicate discrepancies in real-time. Moreover, AI also improves the quality and safety of records, making sure that DMV activities do not contradict state and federal laws and offer smoother and faster access to citizens.
- **Citizen Services:** AI-powered data integration and workflow automation across federal, state, and local agencies help enhance the provision of a wide range of government services to its citizens. Its uses are in the processing of unemployment benefits, the processing of social security claims and the management of public health programs. The AI systems unite the information of various sources, compare it to verify its validity, and automate the processes of work routines, which will allow responding more quickly and precisely to the needs of citizens.

9.4. KEY LESSONS TRANSFERABLE TO U.S. INSURANCE

Cross-industry experience reveals that data integration and interoperability are crucial to decision-making and customer experience improvement. Consolidating disparate data systems into AI-powered pipelines in banking, government, and healthcare helps companies understand their businesses and consumers. In U.S. insurance, the same methodologies can be used to administer policies and manage claims for real-time insights, greater risk assessment, and more personal client connection. Insurers may simplify, reduce overlaps, and improve operational clarity by harmonising data sources like organised policy records, unstructured claim paperwork, and IoT inputs.

Another lesson can be applied to banking (SEC/FDIC) and healthcare (HIPAA/CMS) industries that require automated regulatory compliance. These industries utilise AI to monitor compliance, assess data accuracy, and provide audit-ready reports to avoid fines and comply with changing legislation. Life and P&C insurers can utilise AI-based skeletons to automate reporting, monitor state and federal insurance rules, and proactively identify compliance issues.

Finally, AI-based fraud detection, operational efficiency, and scalable systems teach insurers. AML, tax fraud detection, and healthcare claim analysis can be adjusted to detect anomalous insurance claims, identify underwriting risk, and prevent fraudulent claims. Automation speeds up service delivery, saves labour, and improves customer happiness across industries.

CHAPTER – 10

Tools, Platforms, And Frameworks

The choice of data stack should be a strategic move on the part of U.S insurance organizations; this has been influenced by data volume, complexity of the system, and size of the organization. Commercial tools such as Informatica CLAIRE or SAS Viya are often preferred by large insurers with legacy infrastructure and seek significant ETL functionality, high-end support and sophisticated analytics integration. These platforms allow automated metadata discovery, anomaly detection, and streamlining workflows, enhancing the efficiency of operational processes in underwriting, claims management, and customer analytics. Smaller insurers and startups, in their turn, may consider cloud-native solutions like AWS Glue, Azure Data Factory, or GCP Dataflow, that provide scalable pay-as-you-use solutions that can work with structured and unstructured data. Cloud-based infrastructure supports real-time data processing, automated pipeline orchestration, and connection with AI/ML services, and thus are best suited to agile environments with changing data requirements.

Also of high importance are regulatory compliance, interoperability, skill requirements, and AI/ML preparedness. NAIC, HIPAA, and state-level reporting standards cover insurance data with stringent requirements and, thus, platforms with automated compliance monitoring increase in administrative load and decrease regulatory risk efforts. The capabilities to integrate are essential to consolidate the legacy policy systems, CRM systems, and IoT or telematics information into single pipelines to provide real-time, accurate insights. In the usability perspective, usability-friendly platforms such as Alteryx and Talend enable users of non-technical backgrounds to conduct advanced analytics and workflow automation, and open-source libraries such as Apache Spark MLlib, spaCy, and Pandas are flexible and scalable but demand advanced programming skills. Finally, the optimal stack would be a balance of cost, scalability, compliance, interoperability and AI/ML that makes insurers optimize their decision-making, advance predictive modeling, further develop fraud detection, and provide personalized, data-driven services to policyholders.

10.1. COMMERCIAL PLATFORMS IN THE U.S.: INFORMATICA CLAIRE, TALEND, ALTERYX, SAS VIYA

U.S. insurers use AI-driven data management and analytics systems, e.g., Informatica CLAIRE, Talend, Alteryx, and SAS Viya to improve ETL workflows, data quality, and efficiency. Informatica CLAIRE automated metadata discovery, anomaly detection and workflow optimization, regulatory compliance and decision-making in underwriting, claims and customer analytics. Alteryx integrates data preparation, analytics and automation to predictive models, fraud information, customer segmentation and predictive modeling with faster insights without deep technical knowledge. SAS Viya is scalable advanced analytics and machine learning that is used to actuary model, predict risk and optimize claims to improve pricing accuracy, detecting fraud and transforming personalized policyholder service.

- ***Informatica CLAIRE***

The U.S. insurance companies have been introducing informatica CLAIRE an artificial intelligence-based data management and integration system that has become widely used to accelerate ETL processes and data quality management and governance tasks. The platform uses AI and machine learning to help automate the metadata discovery process, identify anomalies within datasets, and suggest optimized workflows to use in order to process data. The automation features of CLAIR allow a substantial reduction in the role of man and fastens the process of integrating fragmented information and signals of several systems, including policy administration system, claims records, and customer databases. It also helps in regulatory compliance e.g. NAIC reporting by having a consistent, high-quality data that is easily audited. The predictive insight and smart automation of CLAIRE assist insurers to improve the decision-making process and operational efficiency in underwriting, claims management, and customer analytics.

- ***Talend***

Talend is a full set of ETL and data integration solutions designed to operate in enterprise complex conditions, including insurance. This is because of its visual interface, drag and drop capability and large collection of pre-written connectors that enable insurers to extract, transform, and load data across a broad variety of legacy and contemporary systems. The artificial intelligence-supported services of Talend improve the quality of the data by detecting the presence of duplicate policies, inconsistencies in customer data, and the unstructured databases. Insurers can streamline claims processing, automate workflows in underwriting and keep policies on accurate records with Talend. Automation of routine tasks and the integration of data in real time reduces the operational risks and helps Talend in supporting faster decision-making, as well as, in ensuring that insurers are able to respond swiftly to the market or regulatory changes.

- ***Alteryx***

Alteryx is a flexible platform that integrates data preparation, analytics and automation within the same environment. U.S. insurers count on Alteryx to provide predictive analytics, fraud detection, and customer segmentation without being highly technical. Its drag and drop interface enable business analysts and data experts to create complicated workflows to clean, transform, and model data. E.g. use cases include insurers using Alteryx to create predictive models to score claim risks, detect possible fraudulent claims, and segment policyholders to use those segments in targeted marketing or retention efforts. The automation capabilities of Alteryx enable insurers to create analytic workflows rapidly and with high volume to generate insights on both structured and unstructured data.

- ***SAS Viya***

SAS Viya is a scalable, cloud-based, platform that targets the use of advanced analytics, artificial intelligence, and machine learning applications. SAS Viya is applied in insurance companies to do actuarial modeling, underwriting risk, and in-depth claims analytics. Its high-performance computing environment can be used to process high and diverse data, such as data provided by the IoT devices in telematics, customer services, and historical records of claims. SAS Viya facilitates the construction of complicated predictive and prescriptive models, recognition of new risk trends, and automated decision making by insurers. Using SAS Viya, insurers are able to enhance accuracy in their prices, detect fraud more effectively, optimize their claims processing and finally offer more personalized and responsive services to policyholders without losing regulatory compliance.

10.2. U.S. CLOUD PROVIDERS: AWS GLUE, AZURE DATA FACTORY, GCP DATAFLOW

Adopted by U.S. insurers are cloud-based data integration, transformation, and analytics automated with the help of cloud ETL solutions such as AWS Glue, Azure Data Factory, and GCP Dataflow. Glue supports structured and unstructured data processing in real-time claims and underwriting processes without servers. Data Factory coordinates multicomponent pipelines on-premises and cloud sources, guaranteeing quality of data, compliance with regulations, and efficiency of operations. The Dataflow manages batch and streaming data to support real-time risk scoring, fraud discovery and responsiveness, and enables insurers with consistent and timely insights, predictive modeling, and better customer service.

- **AWS Glue:** AWS Glue is a serverless, fully managed, ETL (Extract, Transform, Load) service that is created to streamline the data preparation and integration into analytics. U.S. insurers use Glue to automate key activities like data discovery, schema mapping, and transformation of a variety of data sets, structured policy records, claims databases, and unstructured communications with customers. The serverless architecture of it does not require the management of the infrastructure and, therefore, insurers can concentrate on data insights instead of operational overhead. To illustrate, insurers can automatically invoke claims processes, refresh policy records, or feed data into predictive models to underwrite and risk-assess, enhancing operational efficiency and regulatory standards.
- **Azure Data Factory:** Azure Data factory is a cloud-based ETL and data integration service offered by Microsoft which enables the insurance companies to coordinate and automate multifaceted data processes across multiple on-premises and cloud-based data sources. Data Factory enables insurance organizations to collect data across old systems, CRM platforms, Internet of Things devices, and telematics streams, and easily integrate them to support analytics and reporting. Ensured quality of data and regulatory compliance, including NAIC reporting and state-

based insurance regulations, is being assisted by Data Factory to facilitate better operation oversight, risk management, and timely customer service response. It is also scalable so that insurers can operate with substantial data volumes without affecting performance.

- **GCP Dataflow:** Dataflow is a managed service that allows the insurers to process both batch and stream data in real-time, in Google Cloud that can process a large amount of data in real-time, including IoT devices, telematics sensors, and continuous claim events. As an example, Dataflow can process the vehicle telematics in driving events to identify dangerous driving or provide damage in the claim handling. The fact that it can process and transform both batch and streaming data also guarantees that insurers have up-to-date insights to make operational decisions, predictive models, and engage customers in addition to enhancing efficiency and reducing their response time.

10.3. OPEN-SOURCE LIBRARIES: APACHE SPARK MLLIB, DEDUPE, SPACY, PANDAS

Open-source applications, such as Apache Spark MLlib, Dedupe, spaCy, and Pandas, are used by U.S. insurers to improve their analytics and operations. Spark MLlib can be used to perform scalable machine learning in risk assessment, claims prediction and fraud detection. Dedupe eliminates overlapping records to preserve the quality of data and compliance. spaCy extracts and categorizes insights in unstructured text, enhancing the quality of claims processing and customer service. Pandas can clean, analyze and report mid-size datasets, used to support trends, dashboards and machine learning workflow preparation.

❖ *Apache Spark MLlib*

Apache Spark MLlib is a free, distributed machine learning library, which processes and analyzes large-scale datasets. U.S. insurers use MLlib to create predictive models across many applications, such as approximating the likelihood of a claim, modeling underwriting risk, and real-time detection of potentially fraudulent claims. Its distributed computing platform can be used to process large amounts of policy, claims, and customer data in parallel, which makes it specifically appropriate with the enterprise-level insurance data. The use of Spark MLlib by insurance companies in their analytics pipelines allows them to conduct scalable predictive analytics, better risk assessment, and decision-making processes at the expense of lessening computational bottlenecks because of conventional machine learning tools.

❖ *Dedupe*

Dedupe is an open-source Python software that is focused on entity resolution that is essential in ensuring the maintenance of accurate and consistent insurance records. Dedupe is frequently used by insurance companies to detect and remove duplicate records of policyholders, consolidate customer profiles in more than one database, and guarantee data integrity in reporting and analytics. Dedupe will reduce insurers making over-payments on claims, mis-estimating risks, and complying with regulatory reporting requirements by eliminating duplicate entries. Using AI-supported probabilistic matching algorithms, it is possible to identify near-duplicates intelligently to enhance the quality of data and efficiency in its operations underwriting, claims processing, and customer relation management.

❖ *SpaCy*

spaCy is an effective natural-language processing (NLP) framework applied to the unstructured text data in order to extract and analyze meaningful information as well as analyze it. Areas of use in the insurance industry include automated claim descriptions, customer emails, transcript of call, and other documents that have a substantial amount of text in them, processed by spaCy. The spaCy-based AI models can categorize claims, identify possible fraud clues, isolate important data points like dates, sums, or insurance policy numbers, and organize customer requests so that they can be answered more quickly. In automating the extraction of insights out of unstructured text, spaCy assists insurers in reducing the manual review workloads, improving fraud detection, improving customer service, and data-driven decision-making in underwriting and claims functions.

❖ *Pandas*

Pandas is a popular Python data analysis, cleaning, and data manipulation library. In insurance applications, Pandas is especially helpful with smaller-scale analytics tasks including trend analysis, reporting, and exploration data analysis. Pandas allow insurers to process machine learning pipelines datasets in advance, compute important metrics, aggregate data, or create control or regulatory reporting dashboards. Its user-friendly data structures, like DataFrames, enable work with tabular insurance data, such as policy record, claims history, and customer demographics. Although not as scalable as distributed libraries such as Spark MLlib, Pandas can still be used as a key component in the insurance analytics process to quickly prototype an idea, test hypotheses, and conduct more detailed analysis of mid-sized datasets.

10.4. CHOOSING THE RIGHT STACK FOR U.S. INSURANCE ORGANIZATIONS

Choosing the appropriate data stack of the U.S. insurance organizations involves a close consideration of a number of technical and operational factors. The scale and sophistication of data handled by the insurer is one of the first factors taken into consideration. Common commercial offerings, like Informatica or SAS Viya, are beneficial to large, established insurers with long legacy systems and high ETL requirements, where support is enterprise grade and the analytics are integrated. On the other hand, smaller insurers or startups are able to take advantage of cloud-native services such as AWS Glue, Azure Data Factory, or GCP Dataflow, which offer scalable, pay-as-you-drive, able to accept dynamic volumes of data and helps to lower the cost of underlying infrastructure. Platform selection must correspond to the present and future expansion of the data to be supported by the organization to maintain performance and flexibility.

The other important issue is regulatory compliance and interoperability among systems. The data of insurance is highly regulated on the federal and state levels, with NAIC reporting, NAIC health information regulations under the HIPAA, and additional state-specific regulations. Automated compliance checks can greatly ease the administrative burden and the threat of regulatory fines, which can be accomplished through platforms that promote automated compliance checks. The ability to integrate is also critical, as insurers frequently use a number of legacy policy administration systems, CRM solutions, and IoT-connected devices (ex: telematics in cars or smart home sensors). A stack that smoothly integrates these sources of data increases operational efficiency, provides consistency in reporting, and enables real-time decision-making.

The requirements of skills, cost-factors, and AI/ML preparedness have to be applied when choosing the platform. Some products such as Alteryx and Talend are targeted at customers with minimal or no coding experience that facilitates faster implementation and lessens the dependency on specialized developers. Alternatively, open-source systems such as Apache Spark MLlib or language-neutral NLP systems such as spaCy are more flexible and scalable but need more advanced Python expertise and more complex engineering support. Insurers need to consider the costs of licensing, the complexity of implementation, and the requirements of scalability and make sure the stack has the predictive analytics to support underwriting, claims fraud detection, and customer behavior modeling. Finally, the optimal stack is regulatory compliance, interoperability, cost-efficiency and AI/ML-readiness to fuel data-driven innovation throughout the organization.

PART-IV

Governance, Talent, And the Road Ahead

CHAPTER – 11

Compliance, Governance, And Data Ethics in The U.S.

Organizations in the highly-regulated U.S. insurance and financial sectors are required to adhere to frameworks, including NAIC, HIPAA, GDPR, and CCPA, which address data integrity, privacy and security. The AI and ETL systems assist in automating compliance through aggregating, validating, and harmonizing the data across various sources to provide an accurate reporting, audit-ready, and regulatory compliance. Explainable AI is becoming more critical because decisions taken in underwriting, claims, and lending by artificial intelligence have serious financial and social consequences. Such methods as SHAP and LIME, interpretable models and appropriate documentation guarantee transparency, reduce legal risks, and lead to consumer trust. Moreover, AI-based bias management is important to avoid discriminatory results in credit approvals, insurance underwriting, and claims processing, and pre-processing, in-processing and post-processing fairness measures, along with ongoing monitoring, are important in equitable and responsible decisions.

The lineage of traceable data and detailed audit trails is essential to prove that it meets the requirements of regulators like NAIC, SEC and IRS. Organizations can demonstrate the accuracy, consistency, and compliance with legal requirements by showing data trace they collected to its origin through transformations that lead to their ultimate reporting or AI-supported choices. The access, changes and outputs of AI models are tracked in audit trails and help in transparency, error detection and internal controls. Technology solutions such as Informatica CLAIRE, Talend, AWS CloudTrail, and Azure Monitor automate lineage tracking, and keep immutable logs, enabling insurers and financial institutions to easily comply with regulatory requirements, reinforce operational accountability, and maintain trust with regulators, stakeholders and customers in addition to improving overall data governance.

11.1. U.S. INDUSTRY REGULATIONS: NAIC, HIPAA, GDPR (CROSS-BORDER), CCPA

The insurers in the U.S. should adhere to the regulatory frameworks such as NAIC, HIPAA, GDPR, and CCPA that regulate data integrity, data privacy, and data security. AI and ETL systems assist in automating the process of NAIC filings data aggregation, validation, and reporting, as well as securing the safety of patient health information due to HIPAA. In cross-border operations, GDPR requires the security of data processing through consent of the EU residents and CCPA provides the residents of California access to their personal information. Compliance in AI pipelines decreases the number of mistakes, lessens the legal risks, ensures audit preparedness, and enhances customer trust.

- ***NAIC (National Association of Insurance Commissioners)***

NAIC is a regulatory, standard-setting group based in the United States, which informs state insurance regulators of the stability, solvency and transparency of the insurance industry as a whole. It sets model laws, regulations and operating guidelines to insurance companies, including such vital areas as solvency requirements, financial reporting and market conduct standards. To the insurers, NAIC standards also demand that they keep accurate, consistent and timely records in various areas of their operations such as in their policy administration, claims and their financial reporting. The systems that are useful in this process are AI and ETL (Extract, Transform, Load). Such systems automate data aggregation among several sources, validate and harmonize data in disparate systems, and facilitate the production of regulatory reports, including Risk-Based Capital (RBC) filings, financial statements, and market conduct reports. Insuring by automating these functions lowers the number of human errors, increases audit readiness and transparency, assuring compliance and allowing regulators to effectively monitor insurer performance.

- ***HIPAA (Health Insurance Portability and Accountability Act)***

HIPAA is a federal law of the United States that is intended to protect the privacy and security of patient health information (PHI) of healthcare providers, payers, and other covered entities. When managing AI systems, data pipelines, and cloud-based storage implementations, medical underwriting, claims adjudication, or healthcare plan administration, HIPAA compliance is a requirement to the insurers. The main protections comprise encryption of PHI during the transit and at rest, rigorous control of access, extensive audit records, and the systems that make sure that AI algorithms do not accidentally disclose sensitive information. Adherence minimizes the likelihood of legal fines, loss of money and publicity. However, AI-based insurance processes need to consider these protections in every bit of data processing, which will guarantee the protection of the health data and keep the operations efficient.

- ***GDPR (General Data Protection Regulation – cross-border)***

Even though GDPR is a rule in the EU, it has a profound effect on the U.S.-based insurers who provide their services to the residents of the EU. GDPR creates high requirements of data protection and privacy, focusing on the legality of data processing, the necessary consent, and the right of the individuals to access, correct, or demand the deletion of their personal data. The cross-border processing of data using AI systems has to meet the requirements through data minimization, pseudonymization, and established data transfer means. As well, consent management systems, detailed audit trail and controls on guaranteeing the respect of individual data rights are essential. Failure to comply subjects' insurers to large penalties and cross-border regulatory disputes, and the global operation, where personal or sensitive data is involved, requires companies to comply with GDPR.

- ***CCPA (California Consumer Privacy Act)***

Among the rights the CCPA gives the California residents are the right to be informed of their personal information, the right to request the cessation of the sale of their personal data, and the right to demand the destruction of their personal information. U.S. insurers that use AI in their marketing, risk, underwriting or claims data management processes will need to incorporate CCPA compliance mechanisms as part of their data pipelines. This involves the transparency, automated consent management, and deletion procedures that enable the California consumers to get their rights into effect. The AI systems will be required to recognize the consumers preferences, automate their requests on opting out or being deleted, and have verifiable records to show their adherence in case of a regulatory audit. These capabilities would help incorporate the legal compliance and at the same time ensuring that the customer trust and operation efficiency are maintained.

11.2. EXPLAINABLE AI IN REGULATED U.S. DOMAINS

AI has an increased burden of transparency in controlled sectors of the U.S. that include insurance and finance. The choices taken by the AI systems, whether in the form of approving loans and the pricing of insurance policies or in refusing claims, may carry a lot of financial and societal consequences to the customers. These automated decisions must have obvious reasons, and regulatory bodies and auditors expect organizations to demonstrate such reasons, because the black-box model that cannot be interpreted might be aligned with legal, ethical and compliance violations. Besides, customers expect greater transparency in the decision-making processes, and explainability is not just a regulatory requirement but a key element in preserving trust in and confidence in AI-driven services.

In order to have explainability, organizations use both technical and procedural methods. The SHAP (Shapley Additive explanations) and LIME (Local Interpretable Model-agnostic Explanations) techniques are common in estimating the impact of individual features on the model outputs giving a good illustration of why a certain decision was arrived at. Where the interpretability of a model is particularly important, the less complex artificial neural networks can be employed, such as a decision tree or a linear regression, as they already provide more understandable reasoning plots. In addition to modeling decisions, model logic, input data and projected results are also documented in ways that create a complete audit trail that can be reviewed by internal and regulatory teams.

The results of the explainable AI implementation are not confined to compliance. Controlling legal and reputational risks of opaque AI systems can be achieved by offering transparent and understandable decision-making processes within organizations. Explainable AI also builds customer confidence, since clients will have a greater likelihood of accepting decisions when the reasons behind them are known. Also, open AI systems assist in internal governance, enabling teams to identify biases, verify model assumptions, and track performance over time, establishing a culture of responsibility and ethical AI use in highly-regulated industries.

11.3. MANAGING BIAS IN AI MODELS FOR FAIR LENDING & INSURANCE PRACTICES

AI applications in lending and insurance are susceptible to biases that may unwillingly discriminate against a shielded category of people, for instance, people of a certain race or gender or a specific age. As these models are frequently trained using historical data, they can also carry with themselves systemic biases of previous decisions, which result in unjust credit granting, interest rates on loans or underwriting insurance policies. These biased results do not only jeopardize ethical values but also subject organizations to regulatory and reputational risks, as the management of bias is also an important factor in the implementation of AI in regulated areas of the United States.

In order to reduce these biases, organizations have strategies at various levels of model development. The emphasis of pre-processing methods lies in the removal of imbalances in training data, like oversampling minority groups or re-weighting samples to minimize historical injustices. In-processing approaches also deploy the use of fairness-conscious algorithms that actively restrict the model behavior to avoid discriminative results in learning. Post-processing strategies modify predictions following the model that has produced outputs, and correct decisions with established fairness goals. All these will contribute to developing AI systems that are fairer and more responsible in their decisions.

Constant checking is necessary to make sure that there is fairness in the long run. The disparate impact, demographic parity and predictive equity metrics can be used by organizations to assess the consistency of AI models to deliver unbiased outcomes to the various groups. Insurers and lenders will be able to detect when biases emerge and adjust models and record compliance initiatives by actively monitoring these measures. Bias management doesn’t merely streamline AI practices with legal standards, including the Equal Credit Opportunity Act (ECOA) and state-specific anti-discrimination laws, but also enhances consumer confidence, making sure that people are treated justly and encouraging ethical adoption of AI usage in the industry.

11.4. CREATING TRACEABLE DATA LINEAGE AND AUDIT TRAILS (SEC & IRS REQUIREMENTS)

Developing lineage of traceable data is a priority to organizations dealing with highly regulated industries like insurance, finance, and taxation. Data lineage is the process of tracing the information back to its source through every transformation, aggregation, and derivation to its ultimate purpose in reporting, model construction, or decision making. In the case of insurers and financial institutions, it is important to keep meticulous lineage in order to prove to regulatory authorities such as NAIC, SEC and IRS.

Audit trails supplement data lineage by documenting all activities of the data, the people who accessed it, or made any changes to it, and the reason why it was changed. Audit trails in the AI-driven environment record model predictions and critical decision-making points, providing transparency to machine-driven operations. Such records are invaluable in regulatory inspections, internal audits, or investigations, allowing auditors and compliance officers to check data process integrity and model deliverables.

Traceable data lineage and audit trails are more than compliance advantages. They encourage the use of root-cause analysis of mistakes or anomalies, improve data governance overall, and establish accountability in areas where choices carry life-changing financial or social consequences. Informatica CLAIRE, Talend, AWS CloudTrail, and Azure Monitor are technologies that help track lineage by automating the process and creating an audit log that cannot be modified, which is simple to verify through visualizations and reporting. By using these platforms, companies can efficiently address regulatory mandates, enhance operational controls, and guarantee the reliability and traceability of operational data as well as AI-generated insights.

CHAPTER – 12

Building Ai-Ready Insurance Organizations in The U.S.

The foundational roles in U.S insurance AI teams include data scientists to create predictive models of underwriting, claims and risk assessment that ensure compliance with regulations; subject matter experts (SMEs) to offer domain knowledge to align AI solutions with real-world operations; and ML Ops engineers to deploy, monitor and maintain scalable, secure, and real-time AI models. The data engineers who maintain ETL pipelines, data governance experts who maintain compliance and audit-readiness, and UX/data visualization experts who convert analytics into business stakeholder actionable insights are examples of supporting roles.

The effective implementation of AI depends on thorough training and organized change management as well. Insurers in the U.S. have also deployed AI literacy initiatives to train employees on the technical, ethical, and regulatory implications of AI, so as to guarantee that employees understand how to interpret model outputs and can use AI tools appropriately. Change management programs will assist in revamping workflows, role clarifications, and resistance, and AI competency can be maintained through ongoing learning programs consisting of workshops, certifications, and in-house training.

The organisation of cross-functional data groups and vendor dependencies are essential to the construction of scalable, compliant AI. Teams integrate technical skills, industry experience and regulatory control with centralized, embedded or hybrid collaboration patterns to strike balance between efficiency, relevance, and compliance. Vendor and platform management entails the choice of tools such as Informatica CLAIRE, Talend, Alteryx, SAS Viya and cloud services (AWS, Azure and GCP) according to technical, integration and compliance needs, and prevents risks such as vendor lock-in or obsolescence. Governance models regulate platform usage, data privacy, and auditability such that AI solutions are productive, safe, and in line with regulatory and operational demands.

12.1. SKILL SETS REQUIRED: DATA SCIENTISTS, SMES, ML OPS ENGINEERS

In insurance in the U.S., AI teams include data scientists who build predictive underwriting, claims, and risk-score models that satisfy regulatory requirements; subject matter experts (SMEs) who offer domain knowledge to ground models to real-world operations; and ML Ops engineers who deploy, monitor and maintain models to provide scalable, secure, and real-time predictions.

- ***Data Scientists***

In the U.S. insurance market, data scientists have a central role in modeling, coding and optimizing predictive models that power the fundamental business processes of underwriting, claims adjudication, risk rating, and customer targeting. They use sophisticated techniques of analytics and machine learning to derive actionable insights out of big amounts of structured and unstructured data, such as policy data, claims data, customer demographic information and external data. Besides technical skills in specific programming languages such as Python and R, and specific structure, such as TensorFlow, Spark MLlib, and scikit-learn, data scientists need to adhere to regulatory frameworks such as NAIC, HIPAA, and CCPA. This makes predictive models to be legal, guard sensitive data and honor consumer privacy. In addition, they consider information visualization tools to analyze the results of a model and share information with business stakeholders to make informed choices and enhance operations.

- ***Subject Matter Experts (SMEs)***

SMEs are experts who are highly skilled in the field of insurance work, rules in the policies, claims processes, actuarial techniques and customer behaviour patterns. They are mainly used to offer the domain knowledge which AI teams can use to create models that best reflect the real-life insurance processing. SMEs make sure that AI and machine learning solutions are consistent with regulatory obligations, with business operations, and that they consider more subtle business scenarios that would be missed by purely technical teams. SMEs are important in closing the technical and insurance operations gap by helping to prove model assumptions, place outputs into context, and making sure that AI systems can work in the service of operational and strategic goals.

- ***ML Ops Engineers***

The deployment, monitoring, and maintenance of AI/ML models in production are the responsibilities of machine learning operations (ML Ops) engineers. They make predictive models and AI pipelines within the insurance industry scalable, secure, and regulatory- and privacy-compliant. Their tasks will also involve the process of integrating models with platforms of claims processing, policy management, vehicle or smart home IoT streams. Such integration allows making decisions in real time and without human interference, e.g. instant triage of claims, dynamic underwriting, and risk scoring. ML Ops engineers keep track of model performance, identify drift and make updates to ensure reliability and accuracy over time, so that AI operations can remain consistent to business needs and regulatory requirements.

➢ **Additional Skills and Roles:**

- **Data Engineers:** Engineer the strong ETL (Extract, Transform, Load) pipelines, handle data inflow of various origin, and provide clean and organized data to inform the model training and operational processes. They are essential to maintaining a stable and scalable data infrastructure to drive AI efforts.
- **Data Governance Specialists:** Enforce regulatory compliance, audit preparedness and enforcing policies: To ensure that the data handling, storage and AI processing comply with legal and industry requirements. Their work ensures that organizations are not subjected to regulatory penalties and their operations are more transparent.
- **UX/Data Visualization Experts:** Translating complex data insights, model results and analytics outputs into coherent, business-actionable visualizations. With AI making its outputs explainable and accessible, such as in predictions, they make it easier to make strategic choices and enables teams to act on predictive insights.

12.2. TRAINING AND CHANGE MANAGEMENT IN U.S. FIRMS

Extensive training programs and organized change management is perceived to be the key to the successful implementation of AI in business activities in U.S. insurance companies. The AI literacy programs form a cornerstone, as it is essential to make employees of all ranks aware of not only the technicality of AI, but also the ethical implication and regulatory opportunities. As an example, underwriters, claims adjusters, and actuaries can be trained to apply AI tools to areas like fraud detection, risk assessment, and optimization of underwriting. Such education will guarantee that the employees are able to properly communicate with AI-based systems, understand the outputs of the models and be able to make appropriate decisions and stay within the regulatory standards, including NAIC, HIPAA, and CCPA.

Change management also plays a significant role in supporting the process of AI adoption since it assumes restructuring the workflow and redefining roles to suit AI-facilitated operations. U.S. insurance companies adopt systematic systems that are aimed at mitigating the unwillingness of the workforce that might be fearful of AI taking over the usual jobs. New procedures, tasks, and decision-making power should be communicated clearly to make the employees more easily adjust, and cross-functional work of business and technical teams can guarantee that the implementation of AI can meet the strategic rest.

Additionally, life-long learning is reinforced to maintain AI skills in the long-term. Organizations promote continuous upskilling measures in the field of AI ethics, explainable AI, and regulatory compliance. This involves their attendance of vendor-conducted workshops, certification, or in-house training specific to insurance professionals. These programs not only increase technical capabilities but also introduce an understanding of the consequences of AI on the wider scope of decision-making that should lead to ethical, transparent, and compliant application of technology to everyday activities. All in all, AI literacy, structured change management, and ongoing learning combined allow U.S. insurers to implement AI successfully without losing the engagement of the workforce and regulatory alignment.

12.3. STRUCTURING CROSS-FUNCTIONAL DATA TEAMS FOR U.S. INSURANCE ENTERPRISES

One of the most important actions of the U.S. insurance enterprises eager to make them AI-ready is to create cross-functional data teams. Such teams are purposely designed to achieve balance in technical skill, industry understanding and regulatory control. The essential staff usually consists of data scientists and machine learning engineers who model and optimize predictive models, as well as data engineers and architects charged with the responsibility of operating data pipelines and maintaining quality data.

The cooperation patterns of such teams may be different based on organizational priorities. With all technical expertise in one team, a centralized AI hub provides the needed standardization of processes, model development, and governance throughout the various business units. Alternatively, embedded model introduces data scientists into individual units, e.g. underwriting or claims, which makes AI solutions quicker to adopt and more in touch with operational requirements. A hybrid model is favored by many organizations: they take the best features of centralized control which guarantees the efficient operation of the organization, but includes domain-specific specialists who make sure the organization is relevant and compliant with various rules and regulations.

Best practices in cross-functional team management underline constant knowledge sharing and openness. Technical and business cross-training can improve both the collaboration and decision-making process as they understand the capabilities of AI and the limitations of its use in the business. It is important to have clear accountability by having ownership of models, data pipelines, and related assets. Further, complete recording of model logic, assumptions, and audit trails creates reproducibility, enables compliance, and builds trust in AI-driven decisions.

12.4. MANAGING VENDOR AND PLATFORM DEPENDENCIES IN THE U.S. MARKET

The vendor and platform dependency management is one of the most important parts of the construction of robust, compliant, and scalable AI capabilities in the U.S. insurance market. Insurers typically use commercial data integration tools (e.g. Informatica CLAIRE, Talend, Alteryx, and SAS Viya), data analytics and AI-based insights, and cloud providers (e.g. AWS, Azure and GCP) to store, compute and generate AI/ML. Selection of vendors is also driven by regulatory compliance needs, integration compatibility with the existing legacy systems and the capacity to support scalable AI and machine learning workloads in addition to technical capabilities. Such considerations guarantee that platforms are capable of managing the sensitive much-volume of insurance information as well as fulfilling the requirements of regulatory authorities like NAIC, HIPAA, and CCPA.

There is more to dependency management than selection of vendors as it aims at reducing risks like vendor lock-in and obsolescence. The hybrid models many insurers pursue is to use commercial solutions with open-source ecosystems such as Spark, Pandas, and MLlib, which help ensure flexibility and avoid excessive dependence on one vendor ecosystem. It is important to revise the use of platforms on a regular basis in order to stay updated with the technological changes and the changing regulatory requirements, to ensure that AI solutions are effective, safe, and in compliance. Governance is core to this process: a series of oversight committees are formed to oversee the relationships with vendors, to impose data privacy and security criteria, and to be auditable. Such a formal governance structure is especially important to the insurers that work with sensitive customer information and claims data because it guarantees that the reliance of the third party does not affect the integrity of operations, compliance with regulations, or consumer trust.

CHAPTER – 13

The Future of AI in Data Transformation

The use of generative AI and large language models (LLMs) is changing U.S. insurers approaches to managing and processing data. Generative AI automates the development, optimization and refactoring of ETL scripts to facilitate faster migration of legacy systems, minimize manual coding bugs and expedite system modernization. With claims and policy administration, AI has the ability to process structured and unstructured data, manage workflows, and extract unnecessary steps, which enhances efficiency and scalability. Likewise, LLMs also help improve metadata enrichment via automatic generation of semantic and context-aware labels on complex data sets, which are crucial to regulatory compliance (e.g., HIPAA, CCPA) and advanced analytics. This lowers the amount of manual work, enhances the quality of data and enables predictive models to use more reliable, practical insights.

Self-reliant data systems, blockchain, internet of things, and real-time analytics also support U.S. insurance activities by empowering end to end automation, real-time monitoring, and prompt decision-making. Autonomous systems clean, convert, and verify big data, preserve high-quality data and minimize operational overhead. Blockchain can offer immutable, auditable policy and claim records whereas IoT devices can provide real-time customer and asset information to be used to dynamically manage risks. Analytics based on real time uses these streams to identify fraud, streamline underwriting and make preemptive interventions. Combined, these technologies enhance operational efficiency, regulatory compliance, and prevent fraud, as well as enhance customer experience and enable insurers to work smarter, faster, and safer in a competitive and data-driven market.

13.1. GENERATIVE AI FOR MAPPING CODE AND ETL SCRIPTS

Generative AI, particularly models based on advanced language architectures like GPT, has shown significant potential in automating the creation, optimization, and refactoring of ETL (Extract, Transform, Load) scripts and other code components essential for data pipelines. In the context of U.S. insurance, this capability allows organizations to modernize legacy systems more efficiently. Traditional ETL development requires extensive manual coding, which is time-consuming and prone to human error. By leveraging generative AI, insurers can automatically produce high-quality scripts that adhere to best practices, enabling faster deployment and smoother integration with contemporary data platforms. This automation reduces the dependency on specialized technical staff for routine coding tasks and accelerates overall system modernization efforts.

In practical terms, generative AI can be applied across multiple insurance processes. For policy administration, AI can generate mapping logic that transfers data from legacy systems to modern platforms, ensuring consistency and accuracy during migration. Similarly, in claims processing, AI can produce ETL scripts that handle both structured and unstructured data, such as PDFs, emails, or scanned documents, thereby reducing manual intervention and minimizing data errors. Beyond data transformation, AI can suggest optimizations in workflows, highlighting redundant steps or opportunities for parallel processing. This ensures that complex insurance operations, which often involve multiple systems and diverse data sources, are executed efficiently and accurately.

The benefits of applying generative AI to code and ETL processes are manifold. Insurers can onboard new data sources more quickly, enabling faster access to critical information for underwriting, risk assessment, and claims analysis. Automated script generation also reduces the likelihood of human errors that can propagate through large-scale datasets, improving data quality and reliability. Furthermore, AI-driven ETL and code automation enhance scalability, allowing organizations to manage ever-growing volumes of insurance data without proportionally increasing technical overhead. Overall, generative AI transforms how U.S. insurers approach data engineering, providing both operational efficiencies and strategic advantages in a competitive, data-driven market.

13.2. LARGE LANGUAGE MODELS IN METADATA ENRICHMENT FOR U.S. DATA

Large Language Models (LLMs) have emerged as a powerful tool for analyzing both structured and unstructured data, enabling organizations to enrich metadata with minimal manual intervention. In the U.S. insurance sector, metadata enrichment is critical for managing vast amounts of complex data across policies, claims, and customer records. LLMs can automatically generate descriptive, semantic metadata, capturing context, relationships, and data quality indicators. By understanding the meaning of textual information and its connections to other data elements, these models help insurers build a more organized, interpretable, and actionable data ecosystem. This significantly reduces the time and effort required for manual tagging, classification, and data annotation.

In practical insurance applications, LLMs are particularly useful in processing policy and claims information. For example, they can analyze unstructured claim notes, adjuster comments, or policy descriptions to generate metadata that captures the underlying meaning, relationships, and context of each record. This enriched metadata supports advanced analytics, predictive modeling, and AI-driven decision-making. Additionally, LLMs help identify sensitive data fields containing personal health information (PHI) or personally identifiable information (PII), ensuring compliance with regulations such as HIPAA and CCPA. By automating these processes, insurers reduce the risk of human error and accelerate the preparation of compliant and high-quality datasets.

The benefits of using LLMs for metadata enrichment extend across operational, regulatory, and strategic domains. Data discovery becomes faster and more intuitive, allowing data scientists and business analysts to locate relevant information efficiently. Enhanced metadata also strengthens regulatory readiness, as sensitive or critical fields are consistently identified and labeled, simplifying reporting and audits. Furthermore, AI and machine learning models built on enriched datasets can leverage more context-aware and semantically accurate information, improving the accuracy of predictive insights and risk assessment. Overall, LLM-driven metadata enrichment provides U.S. insurers with a scalable approach to transforming raw data into meaningful, compliant, and actionable intelligence.

13.3. AUTONOMOUS DATA SYSTEMS FOR INSURANCE AND HEALTHCARE

Autonomous data systems are AI-driven frameworks designed to handle the end-to-end management of data with minimal human intervention. They encompass tasks such as data ingestion, cleansing, transformation, and quality validation, automating processes that traditionally require extensive manual effort. In industries like insurance and healthcare, where data volumes are massive and continuously evolving, these systems enable organizations to maintain high-quality datasets while significantly reducing operational overhead. By automating repetitive and error-prone tasks, autonomous data systems free up skilled personnel to focus on strategic analytics and decision-making, improving both efficiency and accuracy.

In the U.S. insurance sector, autonomous systems play a critical role in claims processing and regulatory compliance. These systems can automatically reconcile claims data from multiple sources, identify anomalies such as duplicate claims or inconsistent entries, and maintain detailed data lineage to ensure traceability for NAIC reporting. By continuously monitoring and correcting data flows, insurers can improve operational efficiency, reduce the risk of compliance violations, and accelerate reporting cycles. This is particularly important for large insurers handling millions of claims annually, where manual data management would be impractical and error-prone.

Healthcare organizations also benefit significantly from autonomous data systems. These systems can integrate data from electronic health records (EHRs), patient monitoring devices, lab results, and insurance claims while maintaining compliance with strict regulations such as HIPAA. Automated cleansing and validation ensure that patient data remains accurate, consistent, and secure, enabling more reliable analytics and informed clinical decision-making. Additionally, these systems can adapt to changes in data formats or the addition of new data sources, reducing the need for constant manual adjustments and supporting scalable health data management.

A major advantage of autonomous data systems across both insurance and healthcare is their ability to create self-optimizing pipelines. These systems can detect schema changes, handle new data sources, and automatically adjust transformation rules without human intervention. This leads to faster analytics, more timely reporting, and reduced operational costs. Furthermore, maintaining comprehensive data lineage and automated quality checks enhances compliance and audit readiness, ensuring that organizations can demonstrate accountability and transparency in data management. Overall, autonomous data systems provide a robust foundation for intelligent, scalable, and compliant data operations in highly regulated U.S. industries.

13.4. INTEGRATION WITH BLOCKCHAIN, IOT, AND REAL-TIME ANALYTICS IN THE U.S.

In the U.S. insurance industry, integrating blockchain, IoT, and real-time analytics enhances security, transparency, and operational efficiency. Blockchain ensures immutable, auditable records for policies, claims, and regulatory reporting, supporting fraud prevention and compliance. IoT devices provide continuous data streams—from telematics, wearables, and smart homes—enabling dynamic underwriting, personalized risk management, and proactive interventions. Real-time analytics processes these streams instantly, allowing rapid fraud detection, event monitoring, and automated responses. Together, these technologies improve pricing accuracy, accelerate claims processing, strengthen fraud prevention, enhance customer experience, and ensure regulatory adherence while optimizing operational performance.

- ***Blockchain Integration***

In the U.S. insurance industry, blockchain technology is increasingly being deployed to provide a secure, decentralized, and immutable ledger for recording insurance contracts, claims, and regulatory reporting. Each transaction on a blockchain is timestamped and cryptographically verified, ensuring data integrity and preventing tampering or unauthorized alterations. This capability is critical for fraud prevention, regulatory compliance, and maintaining trust in insurance operations. Blockchain also improves traceability, enabling insurers to maintain a transparent audit trail for every policy, claim, or financial transaction. Integration with AI-driven data pipelines allows insurers to automate key operational tasks for example, automatically validating that policy conditions are met, triggering claim payouts upon verification, or monitoring compliance in a fully auditable and transparent manner. This combination ensures accuracy, efficiency, and accountability across insurance processes.

- ***IoT Data Streams***

The widespread adoption of Internet of Things (IoT) devices including vehicle telematics, wearable health monitors, and smart home sensors has transformed the way insurers collect and analyze data. IoT devices generate continuous, real-time streams of information about customer behavior, environmental conditions, and asset status. AI-powered data pipelines can ingest and process these data streams at scale, enabling insurers to dynamically adjust underwriting decisions, premium pricing, and risk mitigation strategies. For example, telematics data can monitor driving patterns to reward safe behavior with lower auto insurance premiums, while wearable devices can track health metrics that influence life or health insurance underwriting. Smart home sensors can detect risks like water leaks or fire hazards, prompting preventive interventions. By leveraging IoT data, insurers can shift from static, historical risk assessments to proactive, personalized risk management, improving both pricing accuracy and customer engagement.

- ***Real-Time Analytics***

Real-time analytics allows insurers to extract immediate insights from streaming data, supporting faster, more informed decision-making across underwriting, claims, and operational workflows. It enables rapid detection of suspicious or fraudulent claims, real-time monitoring of catastrophic events like hurricanes or floods, and optimization of internal processes for efficiency. Using event-driven architectures, insurers can automate responses to specific triggers for instance, sending instant alerts to claims teams after severe weather, adjusting policy pricing dynamically based on current risk exposures, or initiating preventive measures for high-risk policyholders. Real-time analytics enhances operational agility, allowing insurers to respond proactively to evolving risks rather than relying solely on historical data.

- ***Benefits***

The integration of blockchain, IoT, and real-time analytics delivers multiple advantages for U.S. insurers. These technologies collectively improve risk modeling and pricing accuracy by incorporating continuous, validated, and high-fidelity data into predictive models. Customer experience is enhanced through personalized offerings, instant notifications, and faster claims resolution. Operational efficiency is strengthened as automated monitoring and immutable blockchain records reduce manual intervention and errors. Fraud detection is also enhanced, as all transactions and data streams are traceable, auditable, and tamper-proof. Overall, these innovations empower insurers to deliver smarter, faster, and more secure services, while maintaining compliance with complex regulatory requirements, improving financial performance, and fostering trust among policyholders.

APPENDICES

Glossary of Key Terms

To support a full understanding of the concepts in this work, below is a glossary of terms frequently referenced in the U.S. context of AI, insurance, and data transformation:

1. **Artificial Intelligence (AI):** Technologies that simulate human intelligence in machines, enabling insurers to automate underwriting, claims processing, and fraud detection.
2. **Machine Learning (ML):** Algorithms that learn from historical and real-time insurance data to predict risk, detect anomalies, and optimize pricing.
3. **Data Mapping:** The process of matching fields from legacy insurance systems to modern platforms, ensuring policy, claims, and billing data remain accurate during migration.
4. **ETL (Extract, Transform, Load):** Traditional data pipeline architecture that collects and processes insurance data. Increasingly replaced by AI-augmented ETL for real-time analytics.
5. **Intelligent Pipelines:** AI-driven data flows that automate schema discovery, anomaly detection, and fraud flagging, ensuring regulatory compliance and operational efficiency.
6. **Telematics:** In auto insurance, the use of connected devices to track driving behavior for usage-based insurance (UBI).
7. **IoT (Internet of Things):** Connected devices such as wearables or smart home sensors that provide insurers with real-time risk data.

8. **Entity Resolution:** AI/ML techniques used to match customers, agents, policies, and claims across fragmented datasets.
9. **Insurtech:** Startups leveraging AI, automation, and cloud-native platforms to disrupt traditional insurance models.
10. **HIPAA/NAIC/SEC/IRS Compliance:** U.S. regulatory frameworks governing healthcare data, solvency, financial reporting, and taxation for insurers.

Sample Data Mapping Template (Life & P&C Use Cases)

Life Insurance Example

- **Source Field:** DOB
- **Target Field:** Date of Birth
- **Transformation Rule:** Standardize format to MM/DD/YYYY
- **Validation:** Cross-check against Social Security Number and policyholder ID

P&C Insurance Example

- **Source Field:** Risk Factor Fire
- **Target Field:** Fire Hazard Indicator
- **Transformation Rule:** Map categorical values (Yes/No → 1/0)
- **Validation:** Verify against property attributes and geospatial hazard data

Insurance Data Migration Playbook

1. **Assessment Phase:** Audit legacy systems (policy, claims, billing) to identify data silos and compliance risks.

2. **Mapping & Schema Discovery:** Use AI/NLP tools to align source and target fields across Life, P&C, and Health systems.
3. **Cleansing & Normalization:** Apply anomaly detection, fuzzy matching, and record consolidation to remove duplicates and standardize SSNs, DOBs, and addresses.
4. **Migration Execution:** Deploy AI-augmented ETL pipelines to extract, transform, and load datasets into cloud-native platforms.
5. **Validation & Compliance Check:** Run test reports against NAIC, HIPAA, SEC, and IRS standards to ensure accuracy.
6. **Post-Migration Optimization:** Monitor with predictive analytics for fraud detection, claims automation, and customer personalization.

Recommended Readings and Tools

Books

1. *Competing in the Age of AI* by Marco Iansiti & Karim Lakhani – Explores AI-driven business models, including insurance use cases.
2. *The Data Warehouse Toolkit* by Ralph Kimball – A practical resource for ETL and data modeling, foundational for insurance migration.
3. *Machine Learning Yearning* by Andrew Ng – Guidance on applying ML techniques in operational systems.

Articles & Reports

1. McKinsey & Company – *"Insurance 2030: The Impact of AI on the Future of Insurance"*

2. Deloitte – *"Modernizing Insurance Core Systems: From Legacy to Cloud"*
3. NAIC – *Cybersecurity Model Law & Data Reporting Standards*

Tools & Platforms

- **AWS Glue / Azure Synapse / Google Dataflow:** Cloud-native AI-driven ETL services.
- **Informatica CLAIRE & Talend:** Widely used for enterprise data integration in U.S. insurance firms.
- **SAS Viya:** AI/ML-driven analytics platform used in actuarial modeling and claims fraud detection.

BIBLIOGRAPHY

1. Akongburo, R. A., Boshe, P., Dei-Tutu, S. A., & Hennemann, M. (Eds.). (2024). *African Data Protection Laws: Regulation, Policy, and Practice* (Vol. 3). Walter de Gruyter GmbH & Co KG.
2. Aksehirli, Z., Bart, Y., Chan, K., & Pauwels, K. (2022). Learn from the Experiences of Others. In *Break the Wall: Why and How to Democratize Digital in Your Business* (pp. 79-145). Emerald Publishing Limited.
3. Akter, S., Michael, K., Uddin, M. R., McCarthy, G., & Rahman, M. (2022). Transforming business using digital innovations: the application of AI, blockchain, cloud and data analytics. Annals of Operations Research, 308(1), 7-39.
4. Annamalah, S., Aravindan, K. L., Ahmed, S., & Sentosa, I. (2025). Exploring the Relevance and Rigour of Case Study Research in Business: A Contemporary Perspective. *Journal of Sustainability Research*, *7*(2).
5. Aziz, S., & Dowling, M. (2019). Machine learning and AI for risk management. *Disrupting finance*, 33-50.
6. Bergset, S., & Nyland, A. J. (2023). *Ensuring safe and secure operations in the norwegian petroleum industry: a study on assessing trends in cyber risk levels* (Master's thesis, NTNU).
7. Bharathan, R. (2025). The Tech Audit Revolution: Navigating the Next 50 Years for Industry and Technology Leadership and An End-to-End Audit Framework for Ads, Search, and Content Platforms.
8. Bhutoria, A. (2022). Personalized education and artificial intelligence in the United States, China, and India: A systematic review using a human-in-the-loop model. *Computers and Education: Artificial Intelligence*, *3*, 100068.

9. Boddu, R., & Lamppu, S. (2024). *Microsoft Unified XDR and SIEM Solution Handbook: Modernize and build a unified SOC platform for future-proof security*. Packt Publishing Ltd.
10. Boinapalli, N. R. (2020). Digital transformation in us industries: Ai as a catalyst for sustainable growth. *NEXG AI Review of America*, *1*(1), 70-84.
11. Brié, B., Stouthuysen, K., & Verdonck, T. (2024). Mandatory csr reporting in europe: A textual analysis of firms' climate disclosure narratives. *Available at SSRN 4231567.*
12. Brock, J. K. U., & Von Wangenheim, F. (2019). Demystifying AI: What digital transformation leaders can teach you about realistic artificial intelligence. *California management review*, *61*(4), 110-134.
13. Bustos, J. P., & Soria, L. L. (2024). *Generative AI Application Integration Patterns: Integrate large language models into your applications*. Packt Publishing Ltd.
14. Butković, L. L., Tomšić, D., & Kaselj, S. (2021). Collaborative strategic view in corporate social responsibility–construction industry case. *Business Systems Research: International journal of the Society for Advancing Innovation and Research in Economy*, *12*(1), 144-163.
15. Chiu, T. K. (2021). A holistic approach to the design of artificial intelligence (AI) education for K-12 schools. *TechTrends*, *65*(5), 796-807.
16. Cohen, M. C. (2025). Digital Disruption in News Media: Evaluating the Canadian Online News Act.
17. Cunningham, R., Barclay, K., Jacobs, B., Sharpe, S., & McClean, N. (2022). Circular Economy Opportunities for the Fisheries and Aquaculture Sector in Australia.
18. D'Costa, C. S. (2025). The Role of AI in the Digital Skill Development of Employees in SMEs.

19. Elci, S., Galindo, M., Rialland, P., & Madhou, M. (2025). Leveraging Science, Technology and Innovation to reduce noncommunicable diseases in Mauritius.
20. Feix, T. (2020). Embedded M&A Strategy. In *End-to-End M&A Process Design: Resilient Business Model Innovation* (pp. 31-107). Wiesbaden: Springer Fachmedien Wiesbaden.
21. Fernando, S. (2022). *A quantitative correlational predictive study of corporate social performance and financial performance*. Grand Canyon University.
22. Feroz, A. K., Zo, H., & Chiravuri, A. (2021). Digital transformation and environmental sustainability: A review and research agenda. *Sustainability*, *13*(3), 1530.
23. Ford, G. (2024). *Non-conformance and rework in construction: a quality management improvement initiative for change* (Doctoral dissertation, Cardiff University).
24. Gottschalk, E. (2024). *Scenario Analysis: A Futuristic Day with Full-Scale Quantum Computing in the Finance Industry* (Master's thesis, Universidade NOVA de Lisboa (Portugal)).
25. Grover, P., Kar, A. K., & Dwivedi, Y. K. (2022). Understanding artificial intelligence adoption in operations management: insights from the review of academic literature and social media discussions. *Annals of Operations Research*, *308*(1), 177-213.
26. Hadziosmanovic, M. (2023). *Corporate climate practices and uses of greenhouse gas reporting: conceptualizing responsibility, filling reporting gaps, and assessing strategic accounting* (Doctoral dissertation, Concordia University).
27. Häkkinen, A., & Koskinen, P. D. J. (2023). *Blockchain in Enterprise Solutions: Assessing the Suitability of Blockchain*

for Corporate Sustainability Reporting (Doctoral dissertation, Master's thesis, University of Turku).

28. Harrison, A., de Nevers, M., & Baird, K. (2025). Transforming Business Education for Sustainability. *California Management Review*, *67*(2), 40-57.
29. Helbing, D. (2018). Societal, economic, ethical and legal challenges of the digital revolution: from big data to deep learning, artificial intelligence, and manipulative technologies. In *Towards digital enlightenment: Essays on the dark and light sides of the digital revolution* (pp. 47-72). Cham: Springer International Publishing.
30. Hennemann, M., Atuguba Akongburo, R., Afua Dei-Tutu, S., & Boshe, P. (2024). African Data Protection Laws: Regulation, Policy, and Practice (p. 215). De Gruyter.
31. I Lyngedal, E. (2025). Leveraging Double Materiality through Life Cycle Principles, ESRS implementation and CSRD compliance.
32. Iyer, S., & Nagaratnam, D. N. (2022). *Hybrid Cloud Security Patterns*. Packt Publishing.
33. Jacq, I. (2025). Combining CSR, Innovativeness and Performance in relation to Sustainability in the Pharmaceutical Industry: Challenges and Best Practices.
34. Janowicz, K., Gao, S., McKenzie, G., Hu, Y., & Bhaduri, B. (2020). GeoAI: spatially explicit artificial intelligence techniques for geographic knowledge discovery and beyond. *International Journal of Geographical Information Science*, *34*(4), 625-636.
35. Kaltenböck, M., Revenko, A., Choukri, K., Boytcheva, S., Lieske, C., Lynn, T., ... & Borg, C. (2023). Deep Dive Data and Knowledge. In *European Language Equality: A Strategic Agenda for Digital Language Equality* (pp. 337-359). Cham: Springer International Publishing.

36. Katiforis, S. (2024). Synchronized Coevolution: A Conceptual Framework For Sustaining a Human-Centered Security Culture in AI-Driven Environments.
37. Kiernan, S. (2024). *A just transition for oil and gas regions? A comparative analysis of just transition policies in Denmark, New Zealand and Scotland* (Doctoral dissertation, University of Victoria).
38. Kraft-Buchman, C., & Peralta, J. S. (2024). Advancing research on feminist artificial intelligence to advance gender equality and inclusion: final technical report.
39. Kruhse-Lehtonen, U., & Hofmann, D. (2020). How to define and execute your data and AI strategy. *Harvard Data Science Review*, *2*(3).
40. Kuzma, S., Bierkens, M. F., Lakshman, S., Luo, T., Saccoccia, L., Sutanudjaja, E. H., & Van Beek, R. (2023). *Aqueduct 4.0: Updated decision-relevant global water risk indicators*. Washington, DC, USA: World Resources Institute.
41. Kwapinski, M. P. (2023). Accelerating Corporate Sustainability by Empowering Individuals: Identifying Value Proposition and Market Gap (Master's thesis, Universidade NOVA de Lisboa (Portugal)).
42. Kwon, T., & Paetzold, F. (2019). Sustainable Investing Capabilities of Private Banks: 3rd Report: Assessment of 20 European Private Banks; 2019.
43. Lee, I., & Perret, B. (2022, June). Preparing high school teachers to integrate AI methods into STEM classrooms. In *Proceedings of the AAAI conference on artificial intelligence* (Vol. 36, No. 11, pp. 12783-12791).
44. Leleux, B., & Van der Kaaij, J. (2018). *Winning sustainability strategies: Finding purpose, driving innovation and executing change*. Springer.

45. Lestari, N., & Xiong, J. Y. (2022). *The Impact of Logistics Provider Data Maturity in Defining Scope 3 Transportation Emissions* (Doctoral dissertation).

46. Lu, Y. (2019). Artificial intelligence: a survey on evolution, models, applications and future trends. *Journal of management analytics*, *6*(1), 1-29.

47. Marcus, L. (2025). *Organizing Process Mining for Business Value* (Doctoral dissertation).

48. Marks, F. F. (2024). *Pivotal or Peripheral: Assessing the Role of Generative Artificial Intelligence in Accelerating Entrepreneurial Success-A Study of Enhancing MVP Development and Product Design* (Master's thesis, Universidade NOVA de Lisboa (Portugal)).

49. Miglani, R. (2023). *Mastering Cloud Storage: Navigating cloud solutions, data security, and cost optimization for seamless digital transformation (English Edition)*. BPB Publications.

50. Mohamed Hashim, M. A., Tlemsani, I., & Matthews, R. (2022). Higher education strategy in digital transformation. *Education and information technologies*, *27*(3), 3171-3195.

51. Mukhamediev, R. I., Popova, Y., Kuchin, Y., Zaitseva, E., Kalimoldayev, A., Symagulov, A., ... & Yelis, M. (2022). Review of artificial intelligence and machine learning technologies: classification, restrictions, opportunities and challenges. *Mathematics*, *10*(15), 2552.

52. Mukherjee, D. V. (2023). *At the edge of tomorrow: unleashing human potential in the AI Era*. Notion Press.

53. Nair, M. M., Tyagi, A. K., & Sreenath, N. (2021, January). The future with industry 4.0 at the core of society 5.0: Open issues, future opportunities and challenges. In *2021 international* *conference on computer communication and informatics (ICCCI)* (pp. 1-7). IEEE.

54. Nandan Prasad, A. (2024). Monitoring and Maintaining Machine Learning Systems. In Introduction to Data Governance for Machine Learning Systems: Fundamental Principles, Critical Practices, and Future Trends (pp. 429-483). Berkeley, CA: Apress.
55. Nelson, A. (2023). *How to Become a Data Analyst: my low-cost, no code roadmap for breaking into tech*. John Wiley & Sons.
56. NOON, U. E. U., & TUESDAY, O. (2021). Environmental, Social and Governance (ESG) Ratings and Data Products Providers.
57. Osterrieder, J. (2024). Generative Artificial Intelligence for Finance Professionals. *Available at SSRN 4956387*.
58. Östgren, G., & Tedroff, H. (2020). Impact Investing in the Residential Real Estate Sector.
59. Paga, P. (2023). *Ethics In Artificial intelligence And Its Impact On Leadership Styles* (Doctoral dissertation, Alliant International University).
60. Panch, T., Szolovits, P., & Atun, R. (2018). Artificial intelligence, machine learning and health systems. *Journal of global health*, *8*(2), 020303.
61. Papalia, L. (2025). *Forensic-Aware DevSecOps Pipeline: Design, Implementation and Execution against a Purposefully Vulnerable Microservice* (Doctoral dissertation, Politecnico di Torino).
62. Parrish, L. (2025). *Security Relationship Management: Leveraging Marketing Concepts to Advance a Cybersecurity Program*. CRC Press.

63. Pencheva, I., Esteve, M., & Mikhaylov, S. J. (2020). Big Data and AI–A transformational shift for government: So, what next for research?. *Public Policy and Administration*, *35*(1), 24-44.

64. Ramaswamy, V. (2025). *The Co-Intelligence Revolution: How Humans and AI Co-Create New Value*. Penguin Random House India Private Limited.

65. Ranjeeta, R. (2025). Beyond Profits: Unraveling the Impact of ESG Initiatives on Firm Valuation.

66. Raschka, S., Patterson, J., & Nolet, C. (2020). Machine learning in python: Main developments and technology trends in data science, machine learning, and artificial intelligence. *Information*, *11*(4), 193.

67. Ribeiro, D. P. M. (2023). *Implementation of a holistic strategy to improve the categorization and management of non-value-adding inventor* (Master's thesis, Universidade do Minho (Portugal)).

68. Ridho, W. F. (2023). An examination of the opportunities and challenges of conversational artificial intelligence in small and medium enterprises. *Review of Business and Economics Studies*, *11*(3), 6-17.

69. Rius, A. (2025). Landscaping industrial policy in Africa: Intersections of industrial policy for sustainable structural transformation.

70. Roestad, C., & Henriksen, S. (2024). *The Board of Director's Innovative Mechanisms* (Master's thesis, NORWEGIAN SCHOOL OF ECONOMICS).

71. Rosales Calderon, O., Tao, L., Abdullah, Z., Moriarty, K., Smolinski, S., Milbrandt, A., ... & Payne, C. (2024). *Sustainable Aviation Fuel (SAF) State-of-Industry Report: State of SAF Production Process* (No. NREL/TP-5100-87802). National Renewable Energy Laboratory (NREL), Golden, CO (United States).

72. Schiff, D. (2025). Strategies for Harmonizing Fragmented AI Ethics Frameworks, Standards, and Regulations. *Standards, and Regulations (June 20, 2025)*.

73. Schweihoff, J., Jussen, I., Dahms, V., Möller, F., & Otto, B. (2023). How to share data online (fast)–a taxonomy of data sharing business models.

74. Seth, N. (2021). *Winning in the digital age: seven building blocks of a successful digital transformation*. Penguin Random House India Private Limited.

75. Sharma, R., Mehta, K., Dhiman, Y., & Shkula, V. K. (2025). Crucial Insights into ESG Reporting: Empowering Sustainable Practices. In Finance, Innovation and Corporate Sustainability (pp. 139-160). Routledge.

76. Singh, S., Madaan, G., Swapna, H. R., Singh, A., Pandey, B. K., George, A. S., & Pandey, D. (2025). Unleashing the power of AI and data analysis: transforming insights into action. In *Interdisciplinary Approaches to AI, Internet of Everything, and Machine Learning* (pp. 1-24). IGI Global Scientific Publishing.

77. Sitty, J. P. G. (2024). *Assessing the Role of Generative Artificial Intelligence in Accelerating Entrepreneurial Success-A Study of the Ideation* (Master's thesis, Universidade NOVA de Lisboa (Portugal)).

78. Sjödin, D., Parida, V., Palmié, M., & Wincent, J. (2021). How AI capabilities enable business model innovation: Scaling AI through co-evolutionary processes and feedback loops. *Journal of Business Research*, *134*, 574-587.

79. Soni, N., Sharma, E. K., Singh, N., & Kapoor, A. (2020). Artificial intelligence in business: from research and innovation to market deployment. *Procedia Computer Science*, *167*, 2200-2210.

80. Steinbrenner, A. S. (2023). *Smart Circularity: Exploring the Impact of Artificial Intelligence on the Circular Economy-Building Block A: Circular Product Design* (Master's thesis, Universidade NOVA de Lisboa (Portugal)).
81. Stirewalt, C. (2022). *Broken news: Why the media rage machine divides America and how to fight back*. Hachette UK.
82. Strazzeri, A. (2024). *Evolving Approaches to Impact Investment: A Focus on European Capital Markets* (Master's thesis, Universidade NOVA de Lisboa (Portugal)).
83. Surampudi, Y. (2024). *Big Data Meets LLMs: A New Era of Incident Monitoring*. Libertatem Media Private Limited.
84. Svempe, L. (2025). The Regulatory Landscape of Health Apps in the European Union. *J. Intell. Prop. Info. Tech. & Elec. Com. L.*, *16*, 24.
85. TAN, K. H. (2025). The Paradox of Technological Displacement: A Novel Framework for Understanding AI and Automation's Impact on Human Capital Development and Labor Market Transformation.
86. te Marvelde, K. (2025). Designing LLM driven tools to support collaboration in complex multi-stakeholder systems.
87. Tran, X. (2024). How Do We Handle Imaginaries? Understanding Audiences and Users Engagement with Perceived Societal Impacts of AI Technologies On Job Displacement.
88. Trigg, S. D. (2025). *Resilience in US-Asia Supply Chains: A Delphi Method Investigation* (Doctoral dissertation, California Southern University).
89. Tyrväinen, D. (2024). How does ESG reporting affect investment decisions by financial institutions? –A case.
90. Valle-Cruz, D., & García-Contreras, R. (2025). Towards AI-driven transformation and smart data management: Emerging

technological change in the public sector value chain. *Public Policy and Administration*, *40*(2), 254-275.

91. Wamba-Taguimdje, S. L., Fosso Wamba, S., Kala Kamdjoug, J. R., & Tchatchouang Wanko, C. E. (2020). Influence of artificial intelligence (AI) on firm performance: the business value of AI-based transformation projects. *Business process management journal*, *26*(7), 1893-1924.
92. Wendelin, F. (2022). How the tech decoupling impacts knowledge management for MNEs.
93. Wewege, L., Lee, J., & Thomsett, M. C. (2020). Disruptions and digital banking trends. *Journal of Applied Finance and Banking*, *10*(6), 15-56.
94. Wilhelm, T. (2025). *Professional penetration testing: Creating and learning in a hacking lab*. Elsevier.
95. Wormald, A., Shah, S. K., Braguinsky, S., & Agarwal, R. (2023). Pioneering digital platform ecosystems: The role of aligned capabilities and motives in shaping key choices and performance outcomes. Strategic Management Journal, 44(7), 1653-1697.
96. Yacus, A. M. (2025). *Response to Disruption and Strategic Logic Blending in Institutionally Complex Mixed Markets: The Adoption & Growth of Online Higher Education* (Doctoral dissertation, University of Massachusetts Lowell).
97. Zerlauth, I. (2022). *Analysis of the impact of green innovation on environmental indicators and the CO2 footprint–Europe's way forward* (Doctoral dissertation, Technische Universität Wien).
98. Zhang, J., & Chen, Z. (2024). Exploring human resource management digital transformation in the digital age. *Journal of the knowledge economy*, *15*(1), 1482-1498.

99. Zhou, J., Li, P., Zhou, Y., Wang, B., Zang, J., & Meng, L. (2018). Toward new-generation intelligent manufacturing. Engineering, 4(1), 11-20

100. Zurawski, J., & Schopf, J. (2023). National Institute of Standards and Technology Requirements (Analysis Report).

Pankaj Pant

Pankaj Pant is a technology leader with over 15 years of experience in data strategy, modernization, and enterprise transformation, with a focus on the Property & Casualty (P&C) insurance industry. He currently serves as a Senior Manager in PwC's Advisory practice, where he leads large-scale cloud, data, and reporting programs that help insurers modernize legacy platforms, improve compliance, and strengthen business performance. Over the years, Pankaj has led several data modernization initiatives from strategy through delivery, helping organizations transform how they manage and use data. He has designed and implemented enterprise data warehouses and reporting platforms for multiple clients, and developed accelerators and frameworks that are now standard across PwC engagements, enhancing both quality and efficiency. His work spans Guidewire systems, data modernization, and applying advanced analytics to solve complex, real-world business challenges. Pankaj holds a Master's degree in Data Science with a specialization in Artificial Intelligence from Northwestern University and a Bachelor's in Electronics and Telecommunication Engineering from the College of Engineering Roorkee. He is also certified in AWS, Azure, and multiple SAFe Agile roles. Pankaj is passionate about finding new ways to use technology for business transformation while contributing to the broader community.

Anshul Kaushik

Anshul Kaushik is a global technology leader whose career has been defined by bold, enterprise-scale transformation across the Life Insurance, Retirement, and Annuities industries. At EY, he drives innovation in technology, data, and AI products, helping organizations harness trusted data, advanced analytics, and artificial intelligence to transform at scale and unlock new avenues of growth. Over the years, Anshul has led sweeping modernization programs that have fundamentally reshaped how insurers and financial institutions operate. His work includes modernizing core life policy administration systems with AI-driven automation, re-engineering underwriting and claims with NLP-enabled capabilities, and migrating retirement and annuity platforms onto modern and cloud ecosystems infused with advanced analytics and predictive insights. With deep expertise in data management, governance, and commercialization, Anshul has established AI-ready data foundations that balance innovation with privacy, security, and integrity. A trusted advisor to C-suite executives worldwide, he has partnered with Chief Data Officers and enterprise leadership teams to design domain-driven governance frameworks that enable both compliance and breakthrough innovation. Widely recognized as an influential voice in the global data and AI community, Anshul's work underscores how disciplined execution, paired with next-generation technologies, can help life insurers and retirement providers not just navigate complexity, but emerge stronger, more resilient, and more innovative.

Satya Prakash

Satya Prakash is a Principal AI/ML Engineer with 18+ years of experience driving enterprise transformation in financial services. He partners with C-suite leaders to shape AI strategy and turn complex problems into measurable outcomes. At Fidelity, he designed an enterprise-grade AI platform for hosting ML models, fine-tuned LLMs, and RAG pipelines, enabling real-time and batch deployments. His GenAI and NLP solutions—call-log summarization, entity extraction, and check-processing automation—have elevated customer service while reducing costs. A proven GenAI leader, he accelerates enterprise adoption and counsels financial institutions on cloud and AI/ML strategy to reduce time-to-value. Known for innovation, integrity, and inclusion, he coaches high-performing teams and embeds a culture of accountability, exploration, and continuous refinement.

Souma Basu

Souma Basu is a Principal Consultant at Capco with nearly 15 years of experience delivering technology, data, and AI-driven transformation programs across financial services. He has guided wealth management, insurance, and banking clients through mergers, platform modernizations, and enterprise data migrations while embedding AI and advanced analytics into day-to-day operations. With a proven record of managing multi-million-dollar consulting portfolios, establishing governance frameworks, and leading diverse cross-functional teams, Souma bridges executive vision with disciplined execution. He is recognized for simplifying complexity, fostering stakeholder alignment, and driving scalable adoption of AI, cloud, and data platforms to generate measurable business outcomes.

9 789368 726852